Fave Art - 15

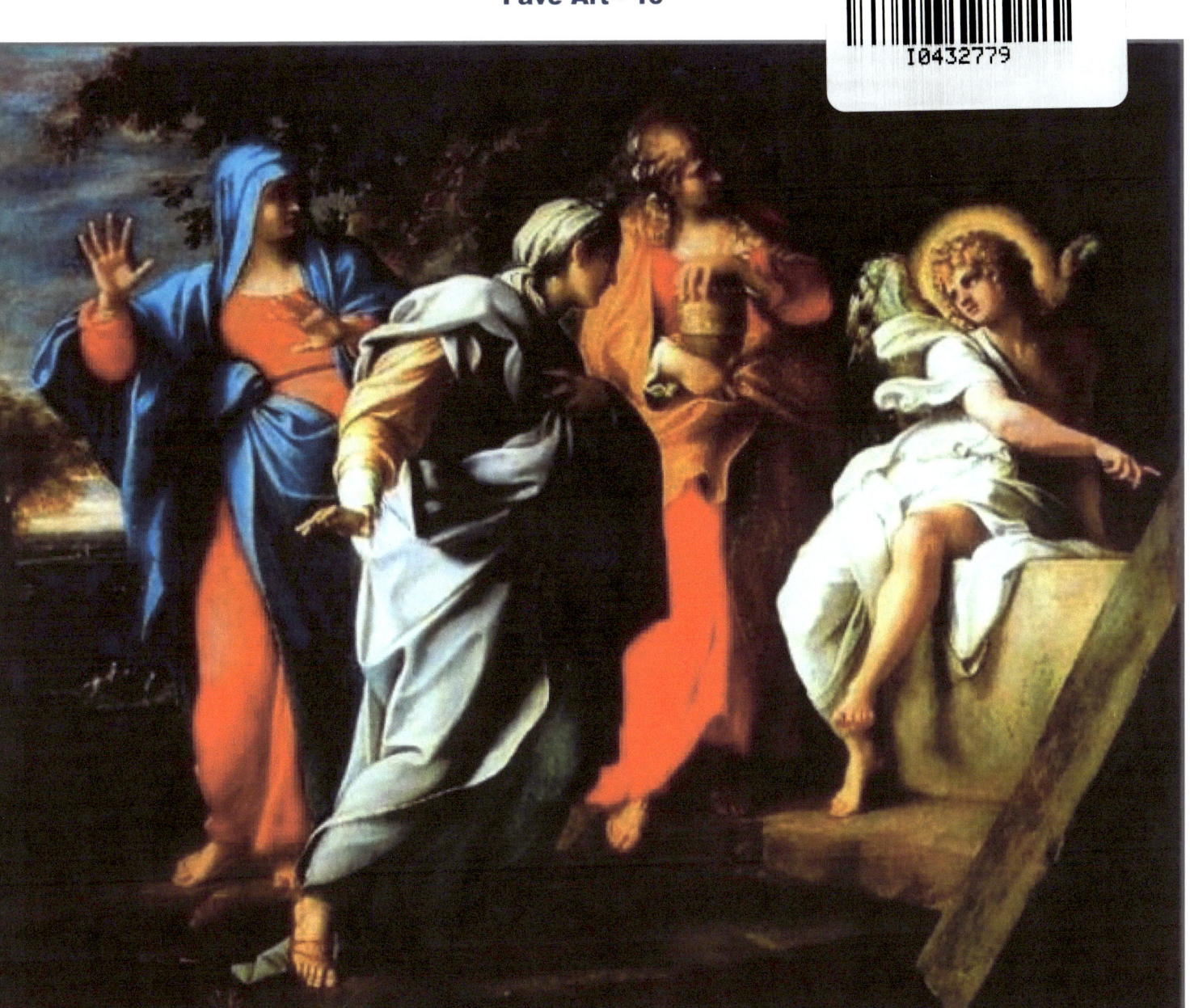

The Three Marys at the Tomb – Renaissance painting

WELCOME! We hope you will enjoy this Fave Art-15 photo album of my favorite random collection of art. Photos are copied from the internet, posters, calendars, cards and art books. You may display this book as coffee table book in your living room, as conversation piece. You may give this as gift. You may cut out each page, 8.5x11 inches, for framing. Printed by Tatay Jobo Elizes under following ISBN Code Numbers:

ISBN-13: 978- 1973822424 & ISBN-10: 1973822423

Printed in USA, 2017. Free to copy by anybody. Why copy? Just obtain the book.

Contact: job_elizes@yahoo.com (Tatay Jobo Elizes, Self-Publisher)

http://tinyurl.com/mj76ccq & http://www.jobelizes6.wix.com/mysite.

Fave Art - 15

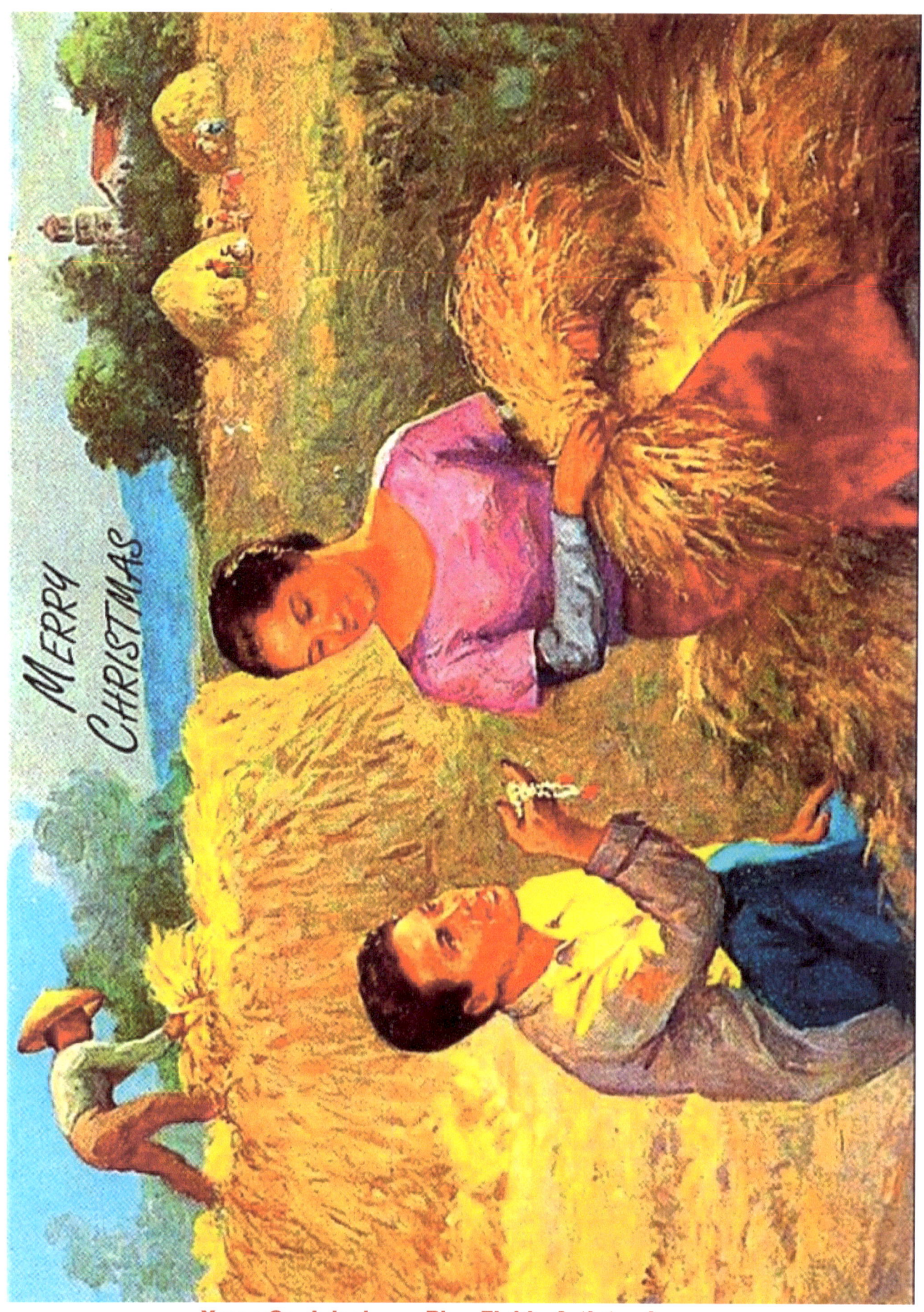

Xmas Card design – Rice Field - Artist unknown

Fave Art - 15

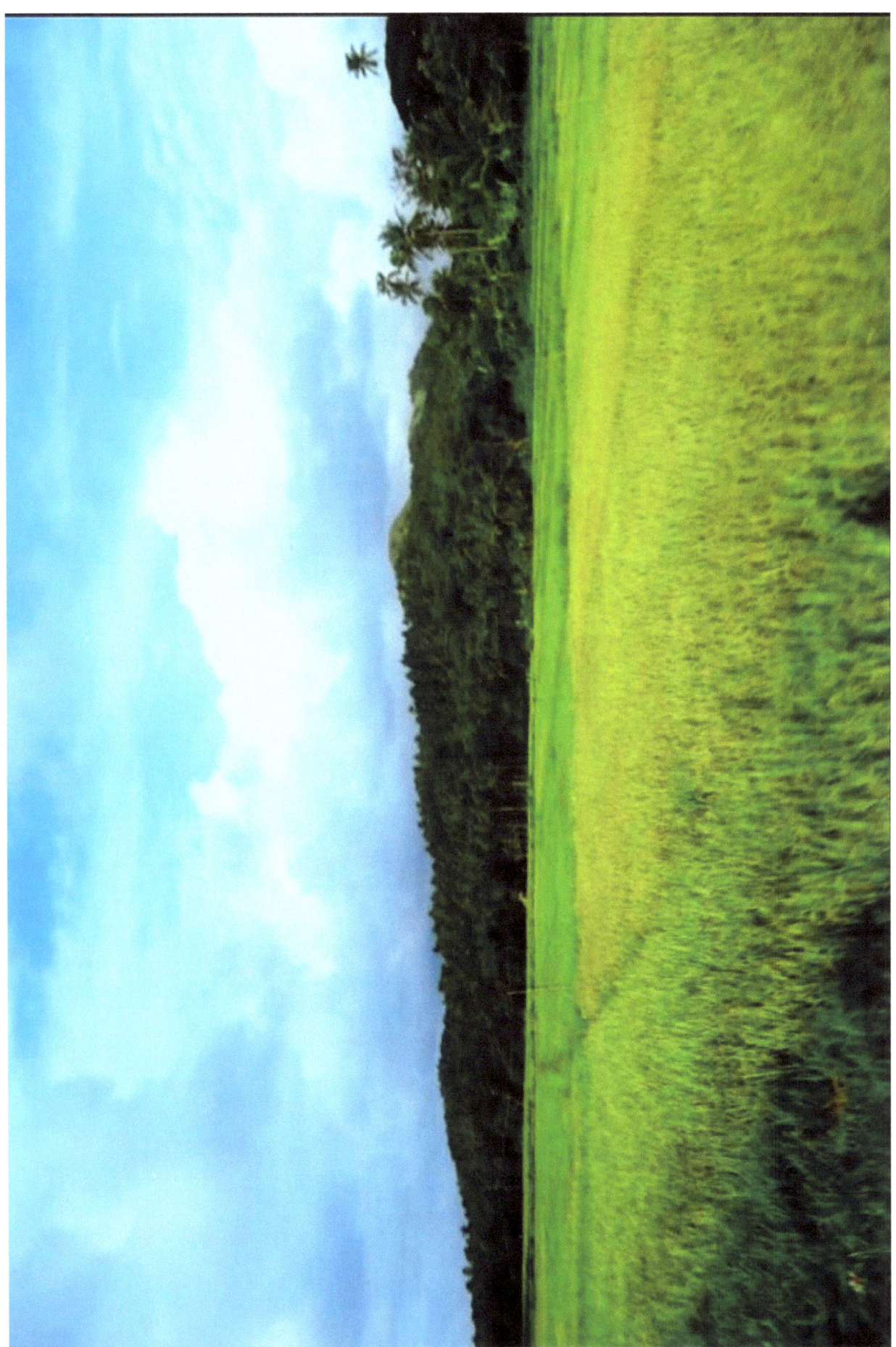

Phil. Rice field – picture, not painting

Fave Art - 15

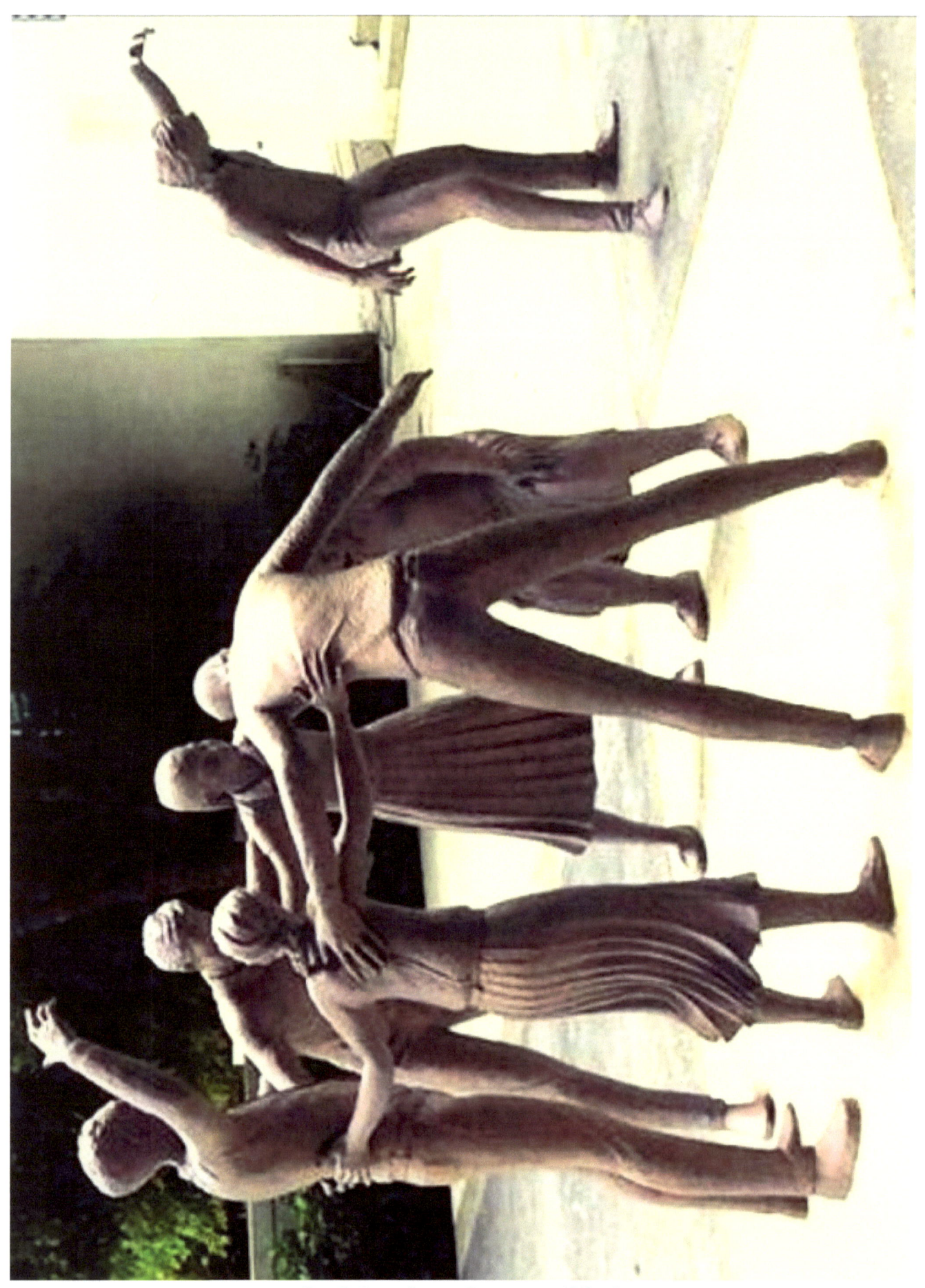

Sculpture in a plaza – untitled

Fave Art - 15

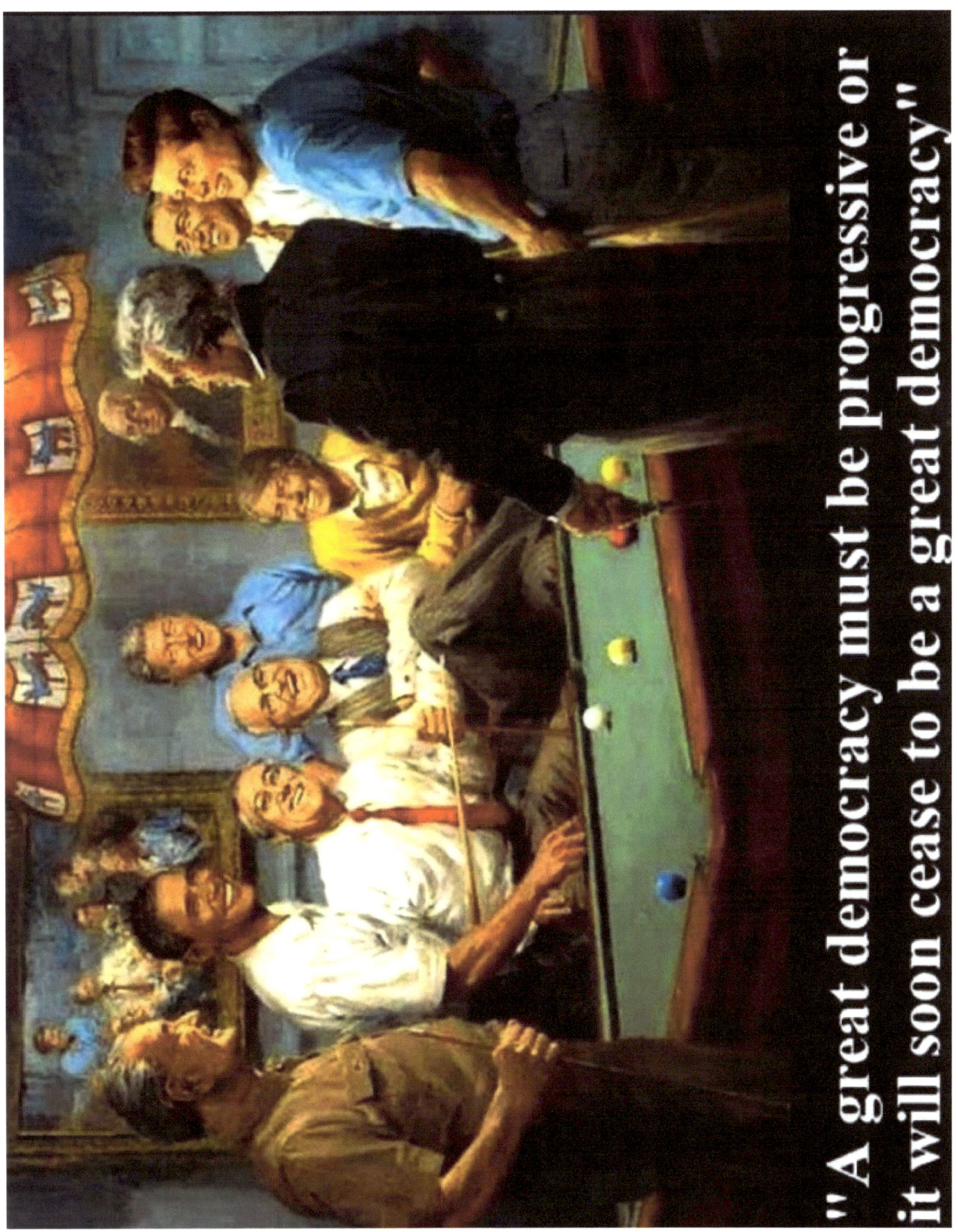

"A great democracy must be progressive or it will soon cease to be a great democracy"

**Poster Design – American Presidents, Democratic Party – L-R, around the table:
Lyndon Johnson+ Barack Obama+ Franklin Roosevelt+ Harry Truman+ Bill Clinton+
Jimmy Carter+ Woodrow Wilson+ John F. Kennedy+ Andrew Jackson**

Fave Art - 15

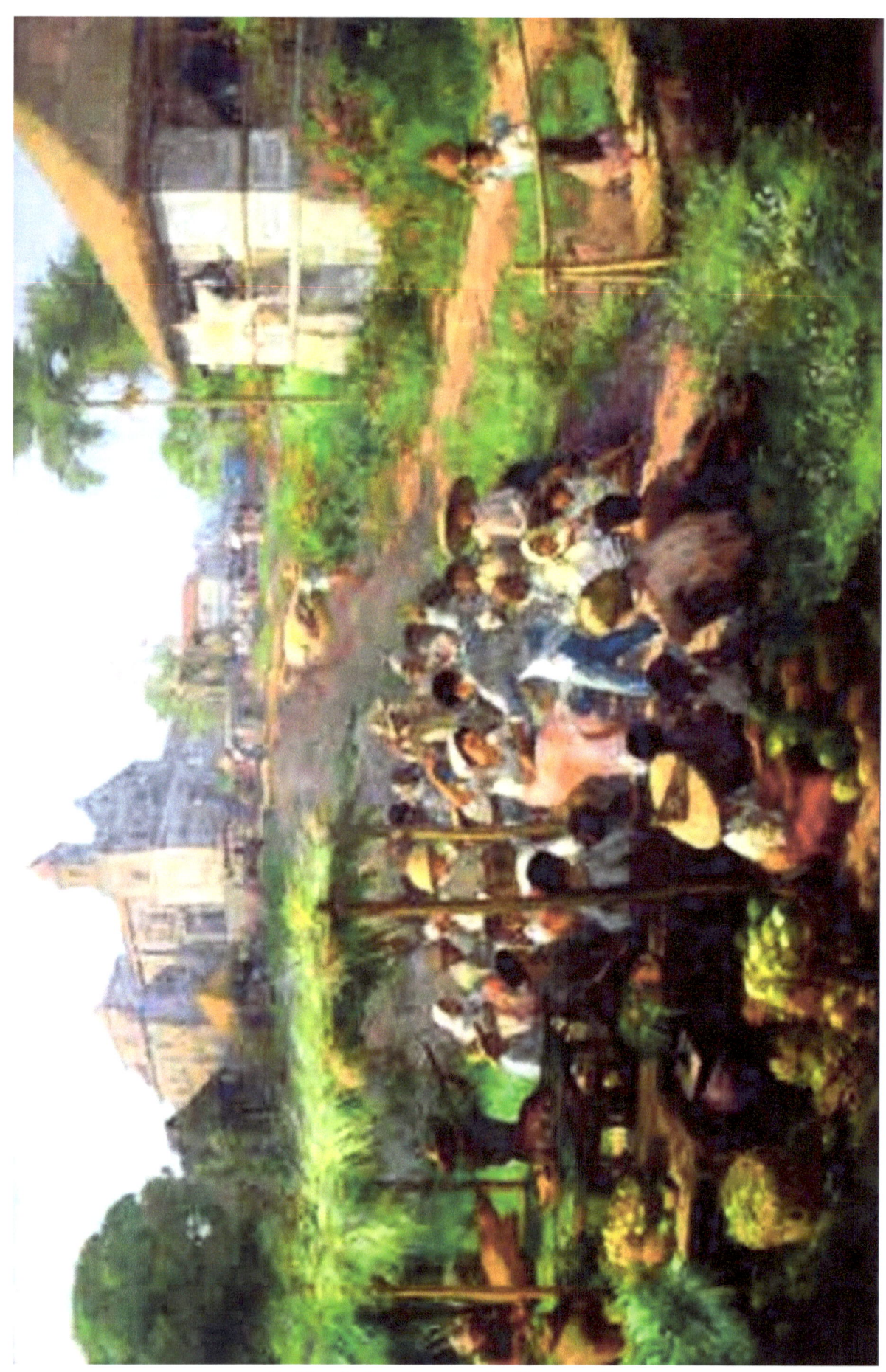

Antipolo by Fernando Amorsolo

Fave Art - 15

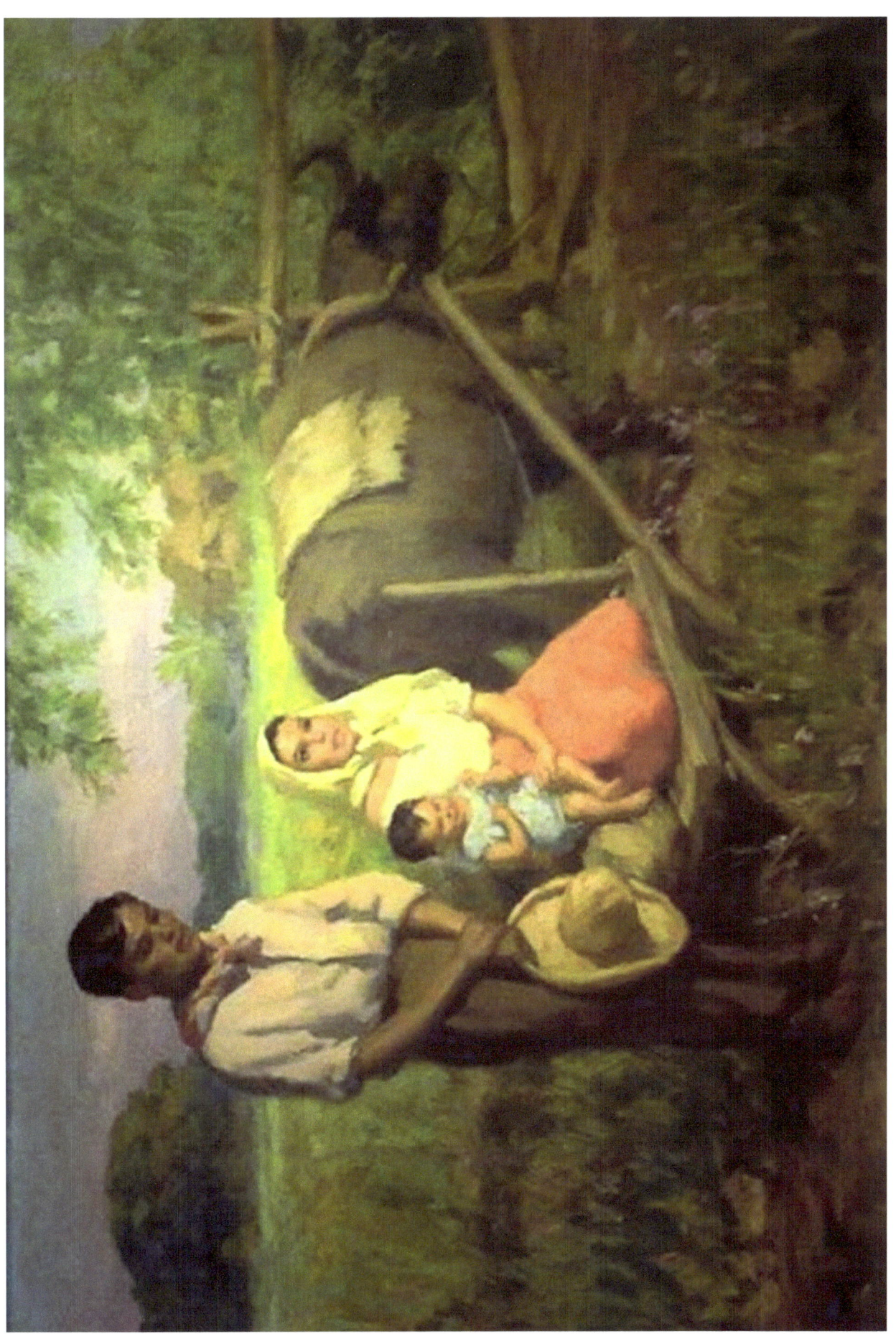

A Rural Family (praying oracion) – by Fernando Amorsolo

Fave Art - 15

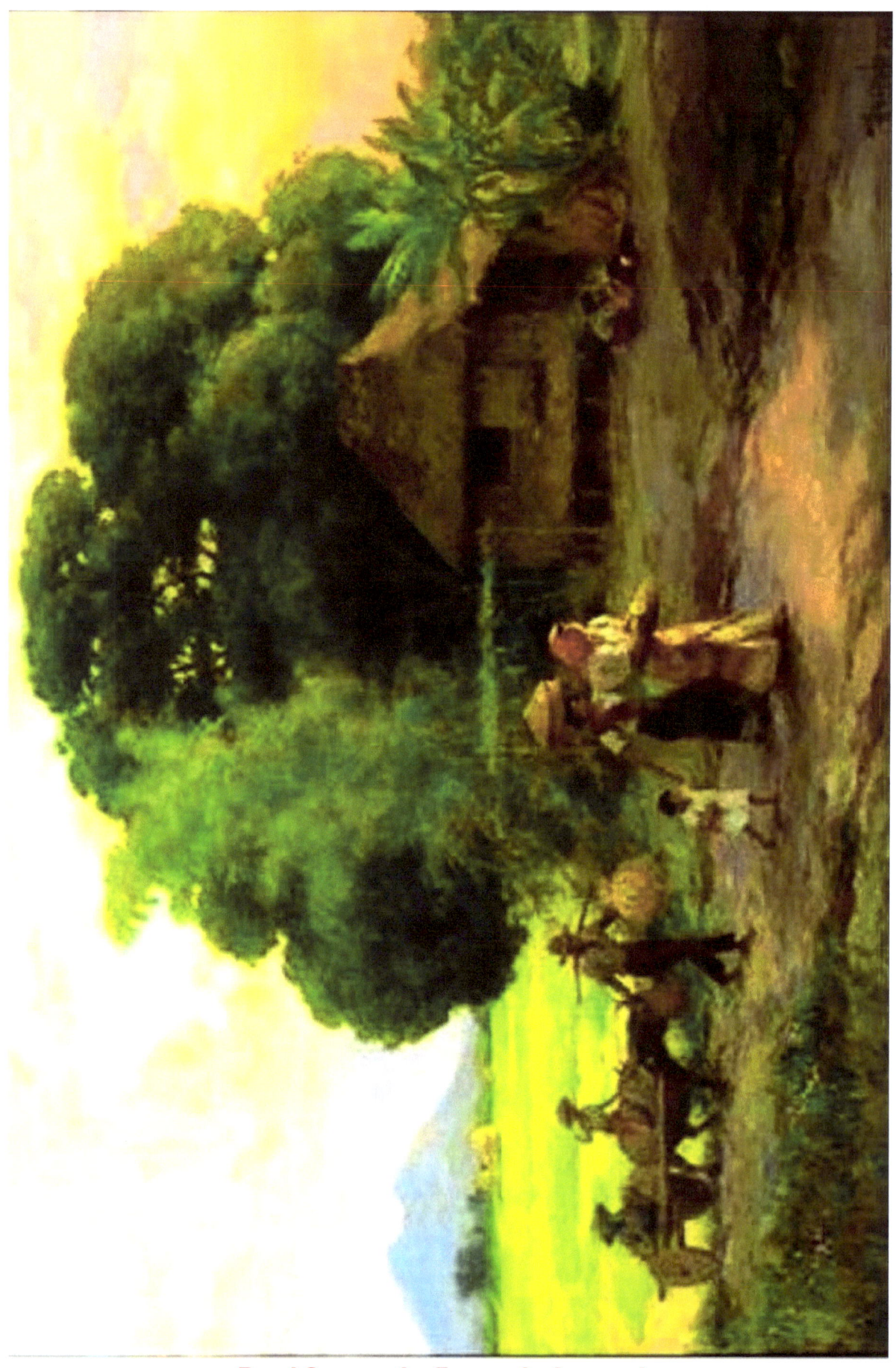

Rural Scene – by Fernando Amorsolo

Fave Art - 15

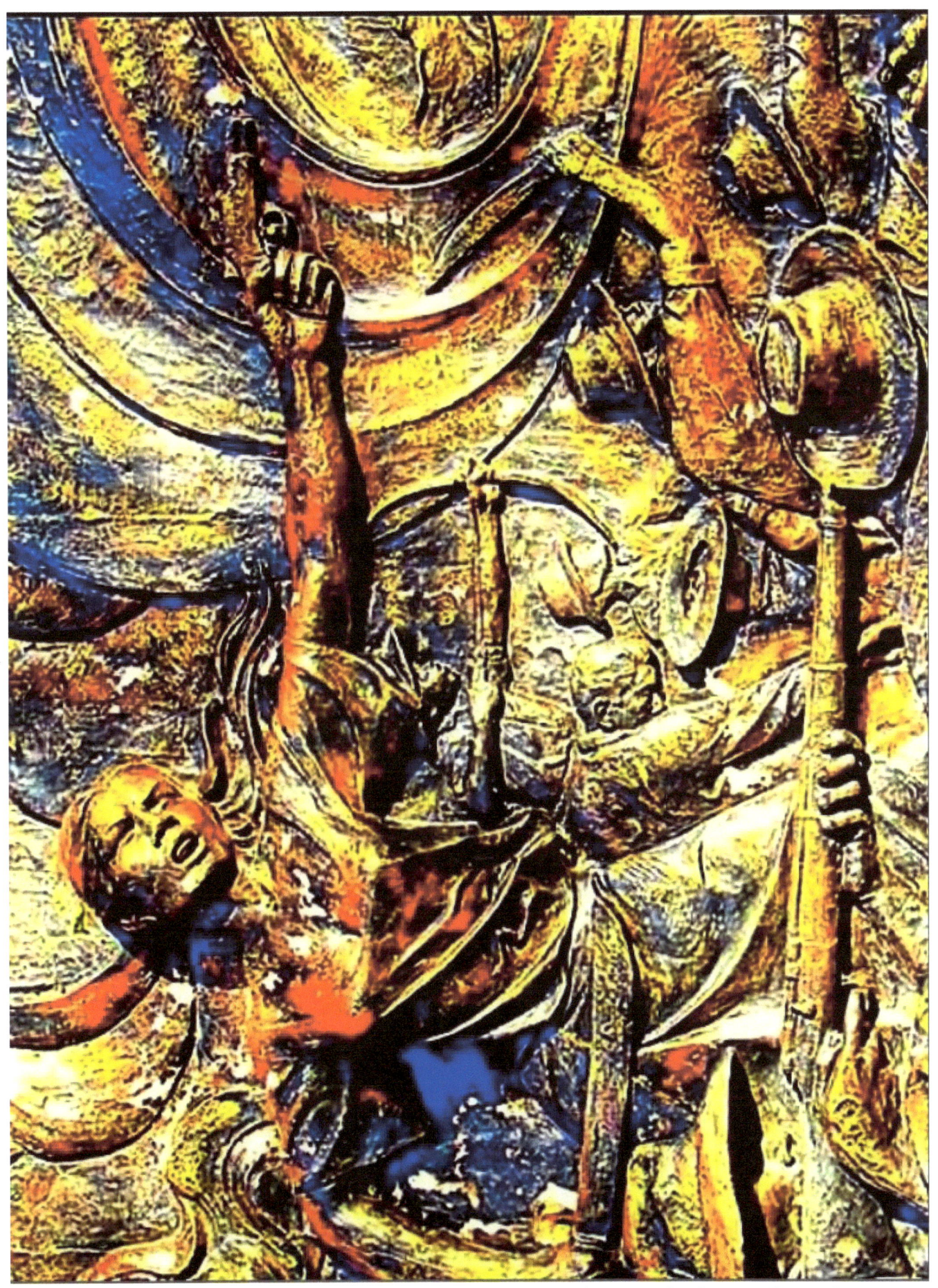

Woman Revolutionary Leader Teresa Magbanua in bronze design, artist unknown

Fave Art - 15

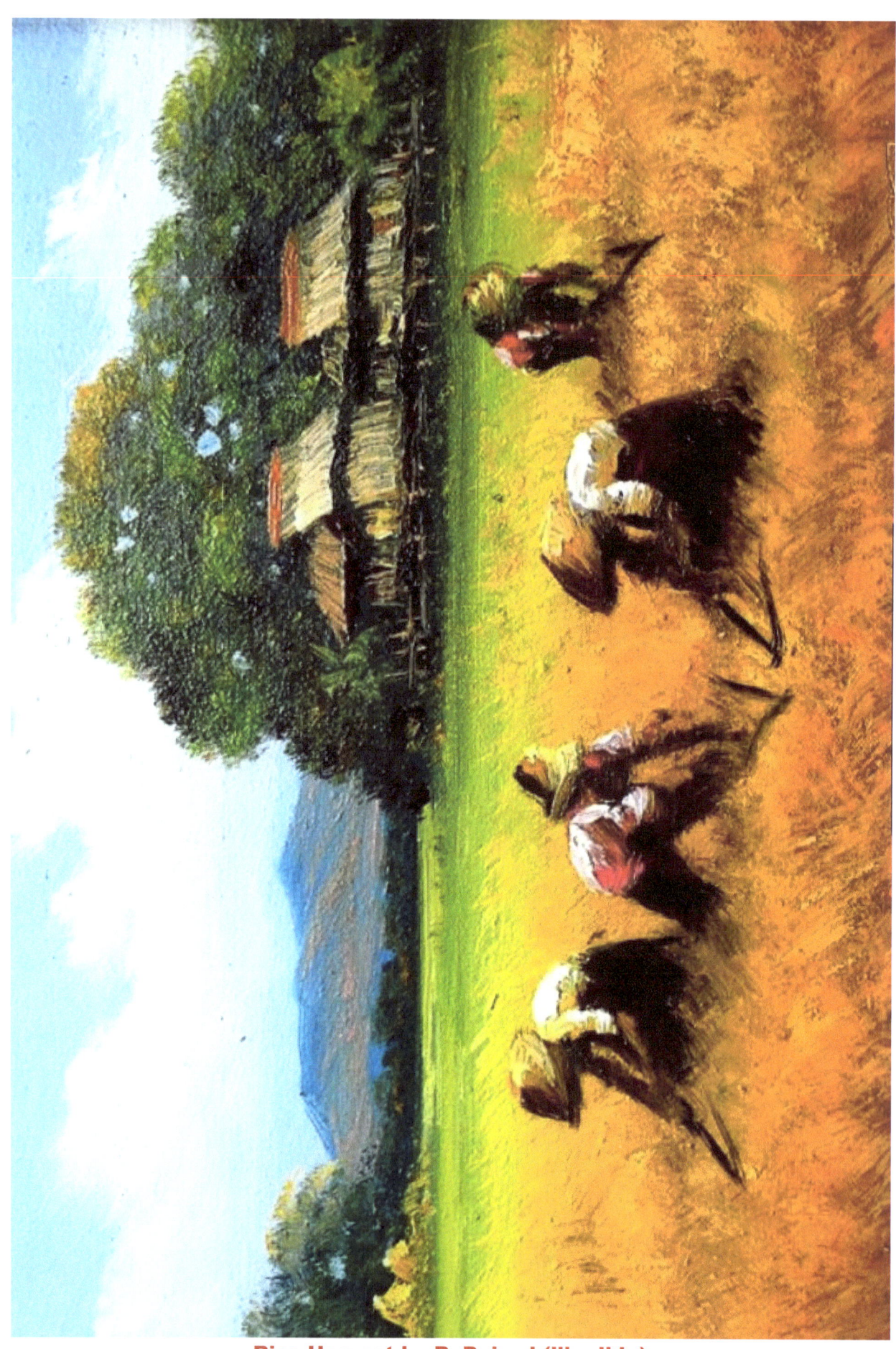

Rice Harvest by R. Poirrol (illegible)

Fave Art - 15

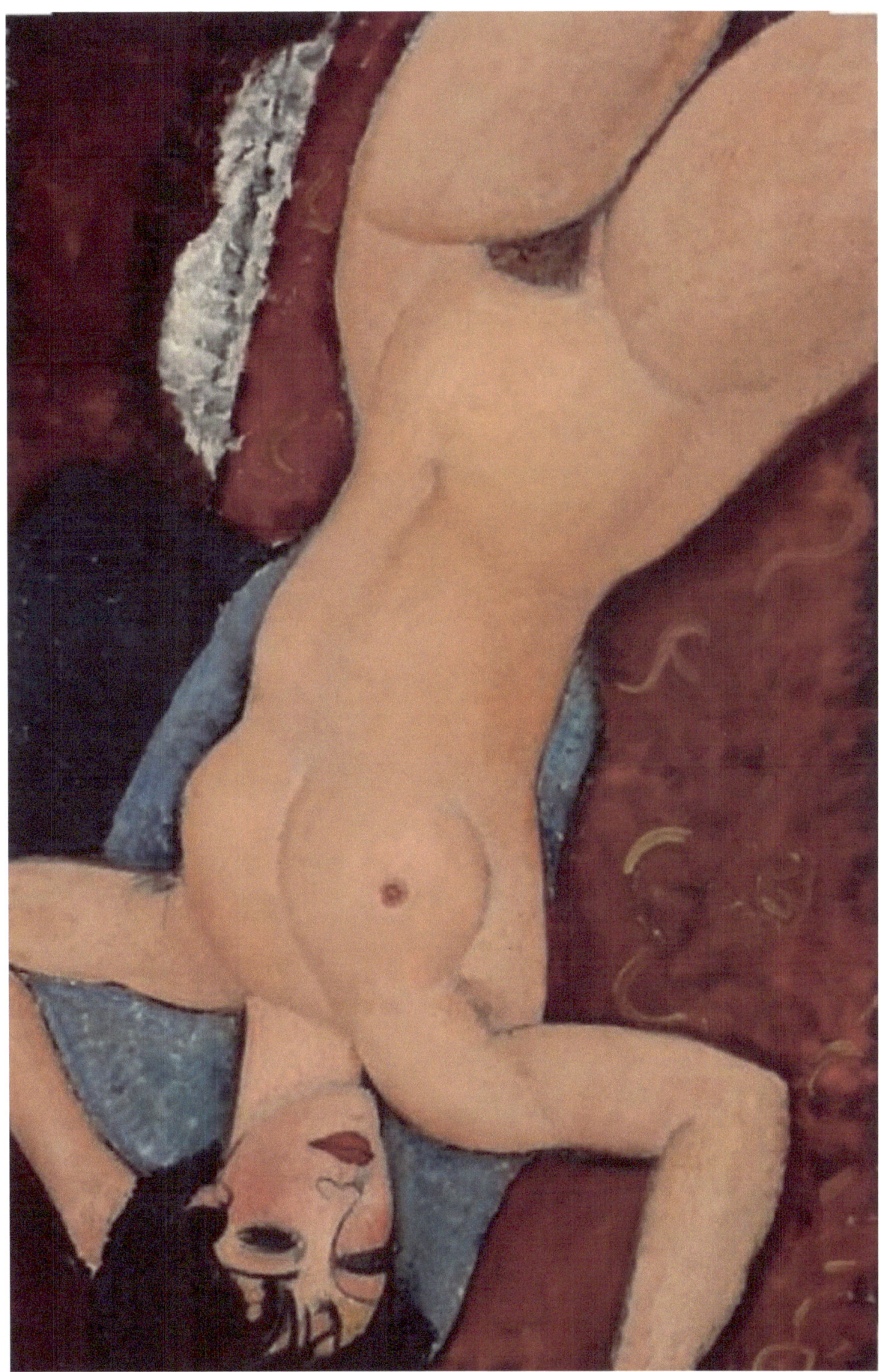

Modigliani's Nu Couche, Sold for English Pounds, 113,000

Fave Art - 15

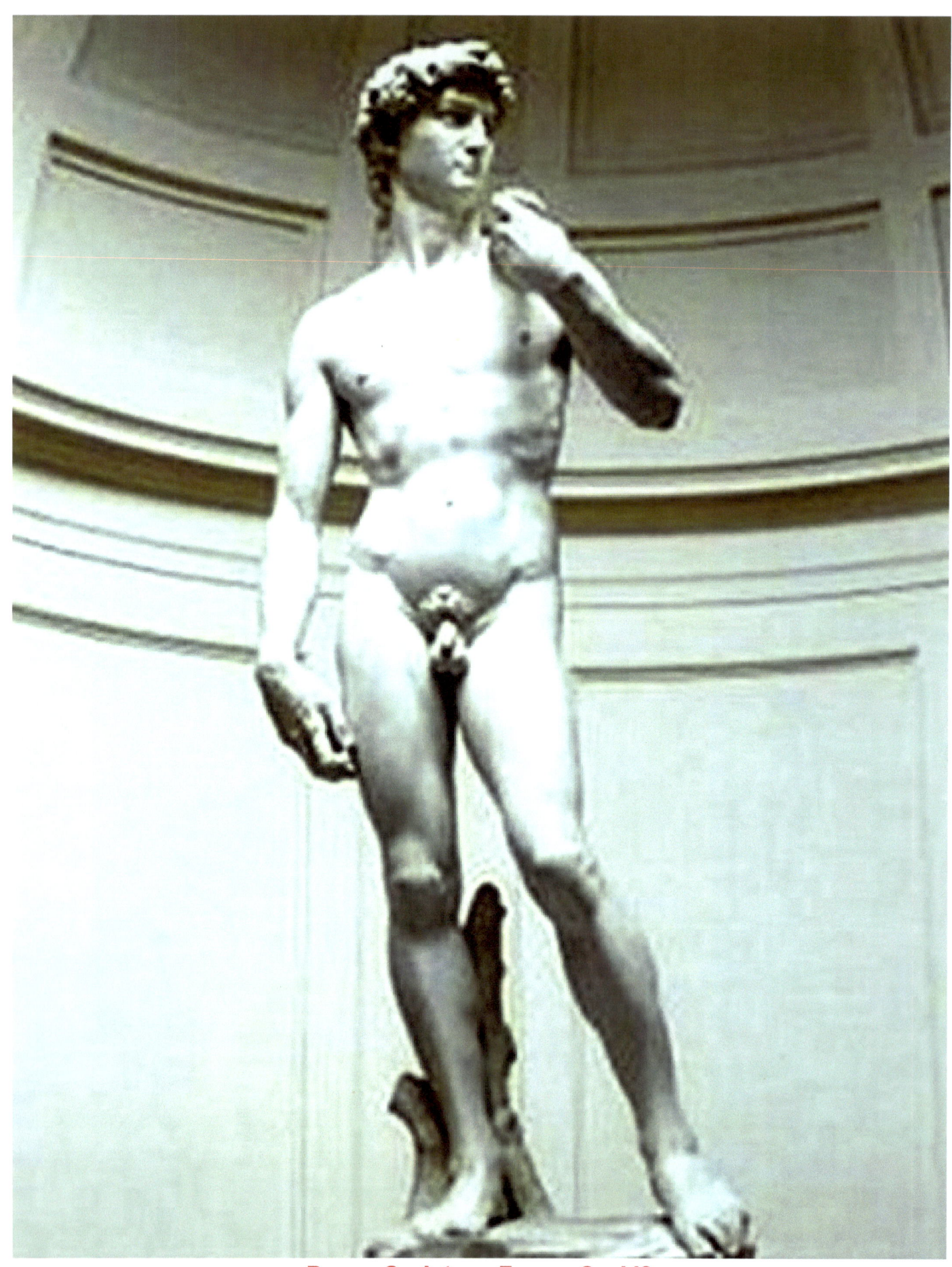

Roman Sculpture, Eros or Cupid?

Fave Art - 15

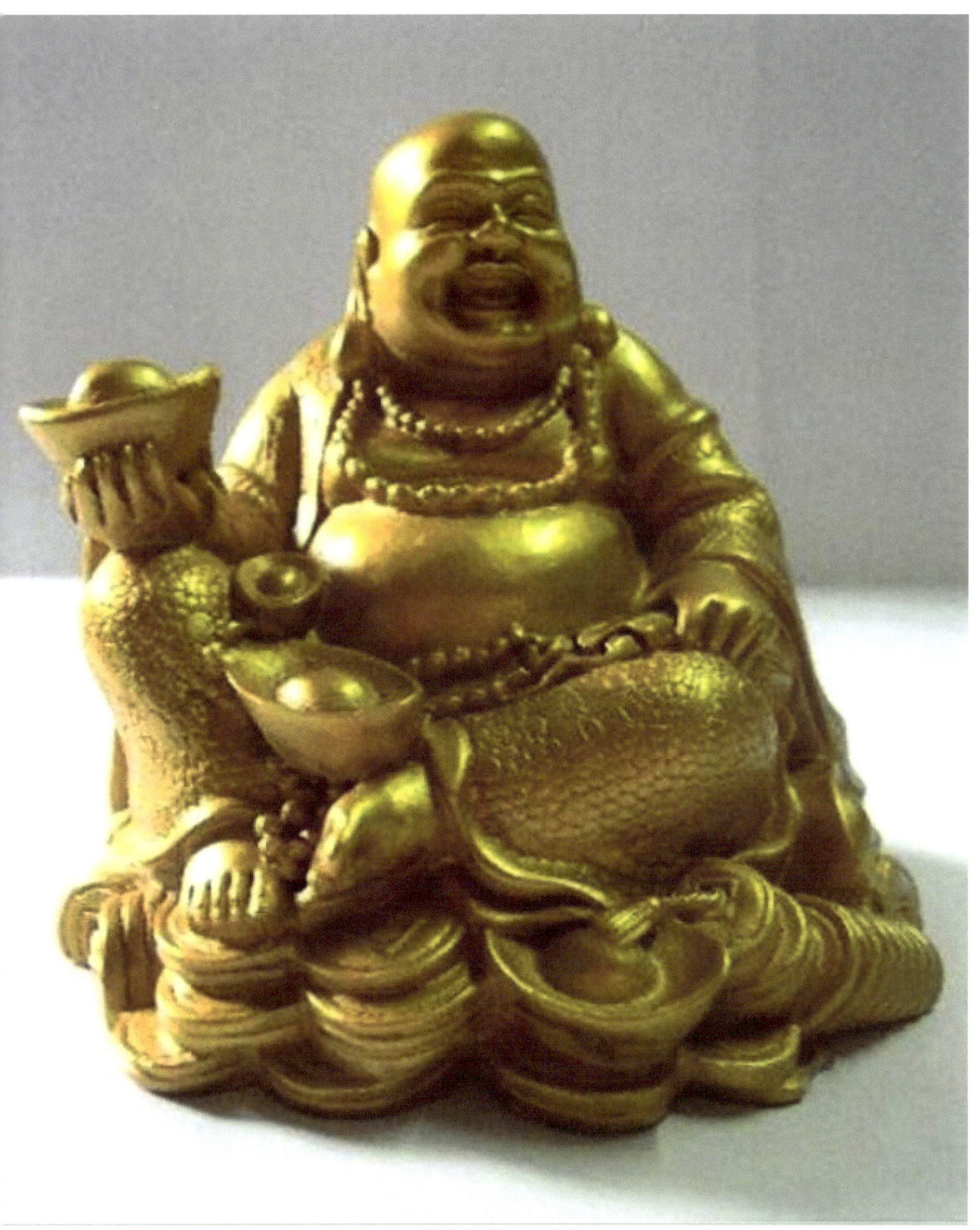

Buddha cast in Gold

Fave Art - 15

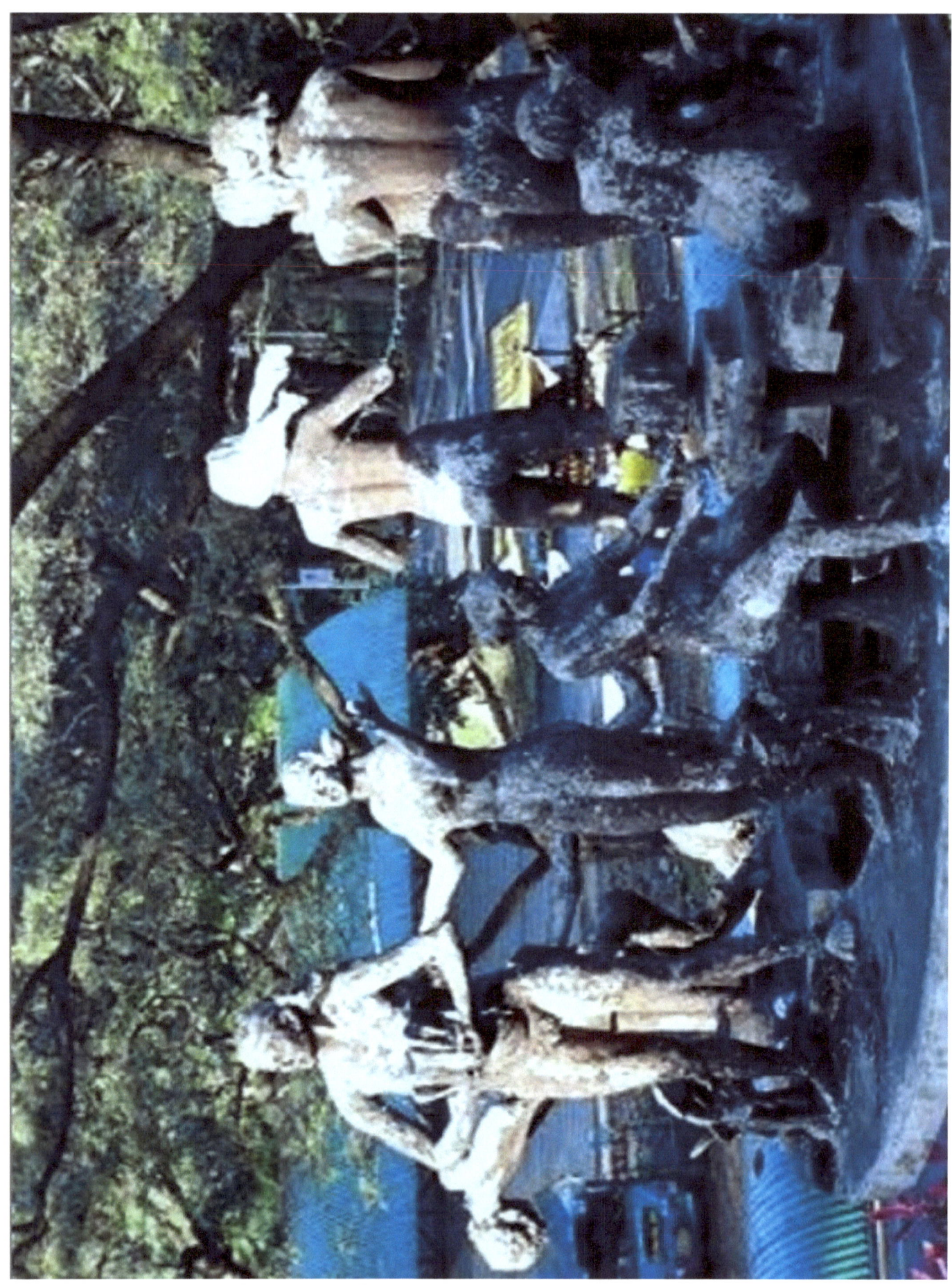

Sculpture of Female Nudes – in a public plaza

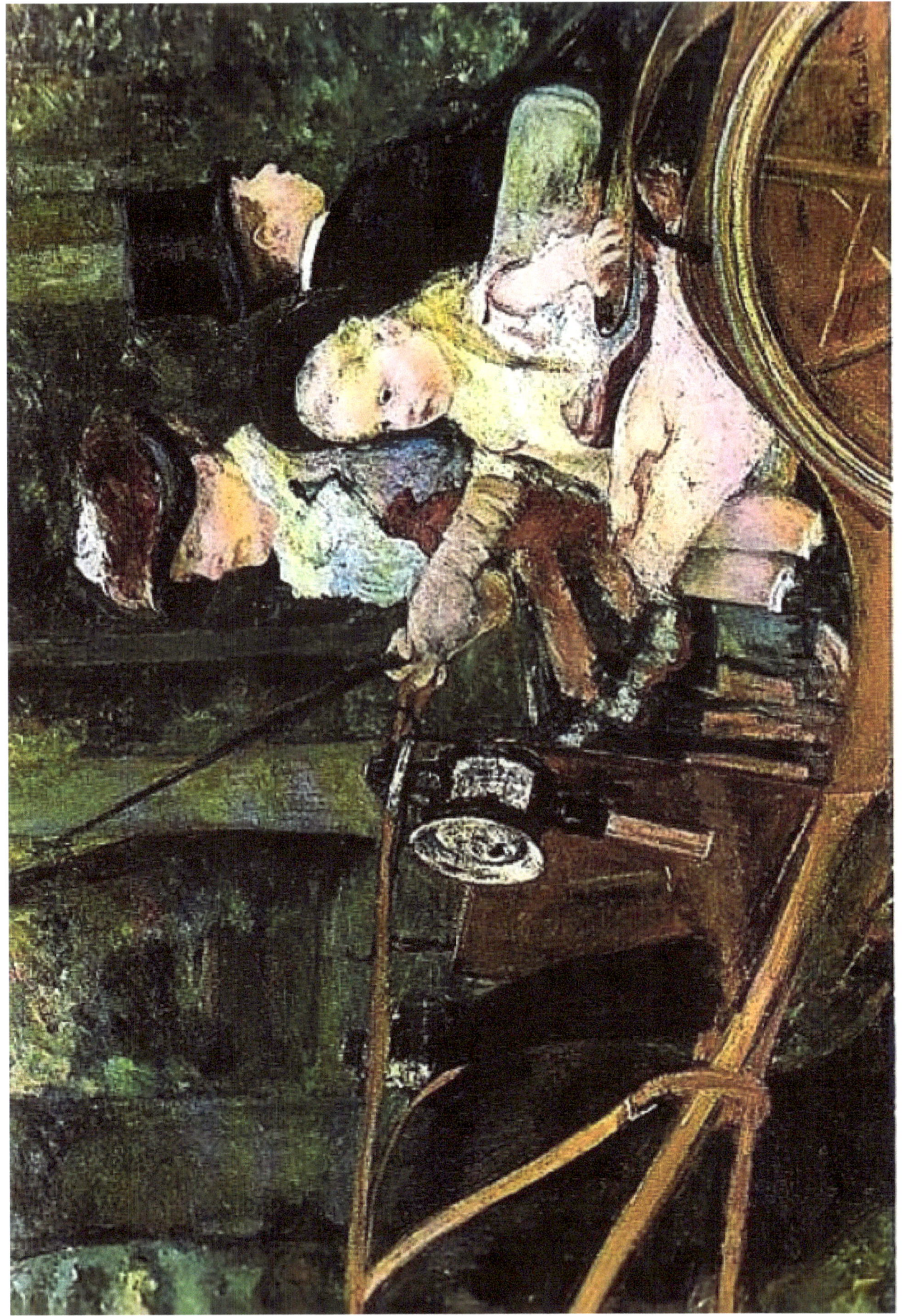

PLATE 47 MARY CASSATT Woman and Girl in the Driver's Seat, 1879 (89.5 × 130.8 cm) Philadelphia, Museum of Art, W. P. Wilstach Collection (Photo: A. J. Wyatt)

A Mary Cassatt Painting

Fave Art - 15

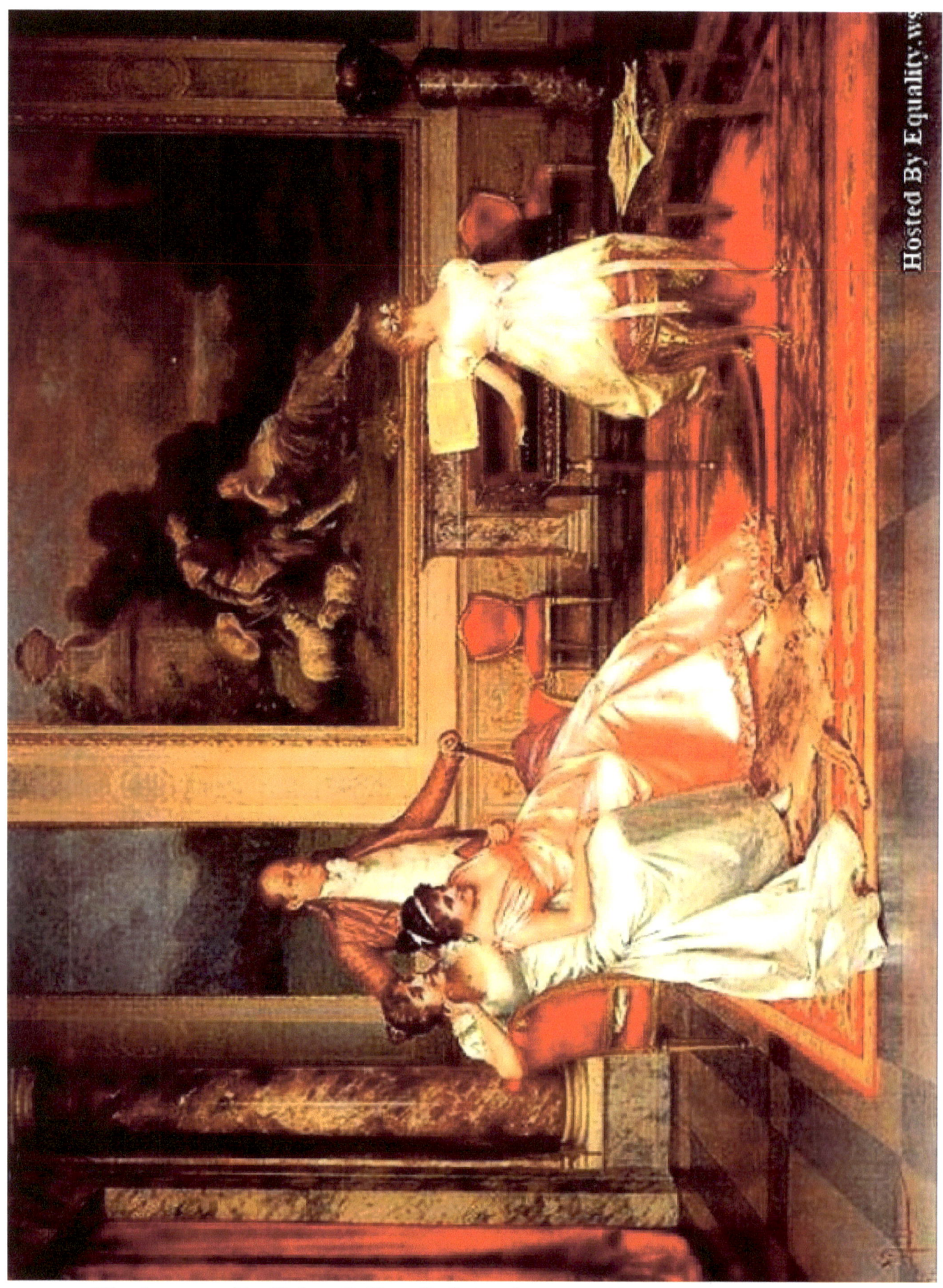

Music room, English painting, Artist unknown – Hosted by Equality.ws

Fave Art - 15

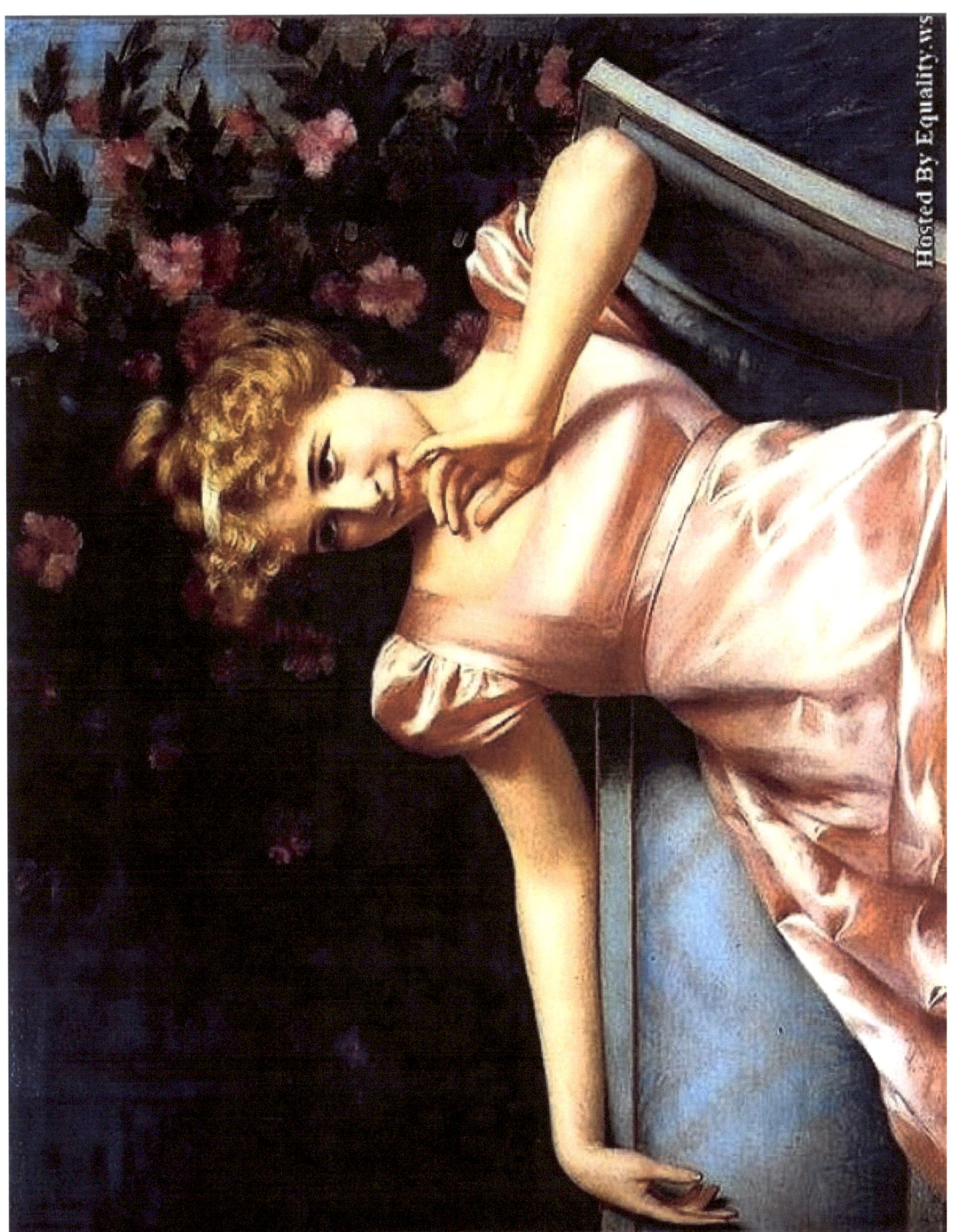

Young Lady – English painting – hosted by Equality.ws

Fave Art - 15

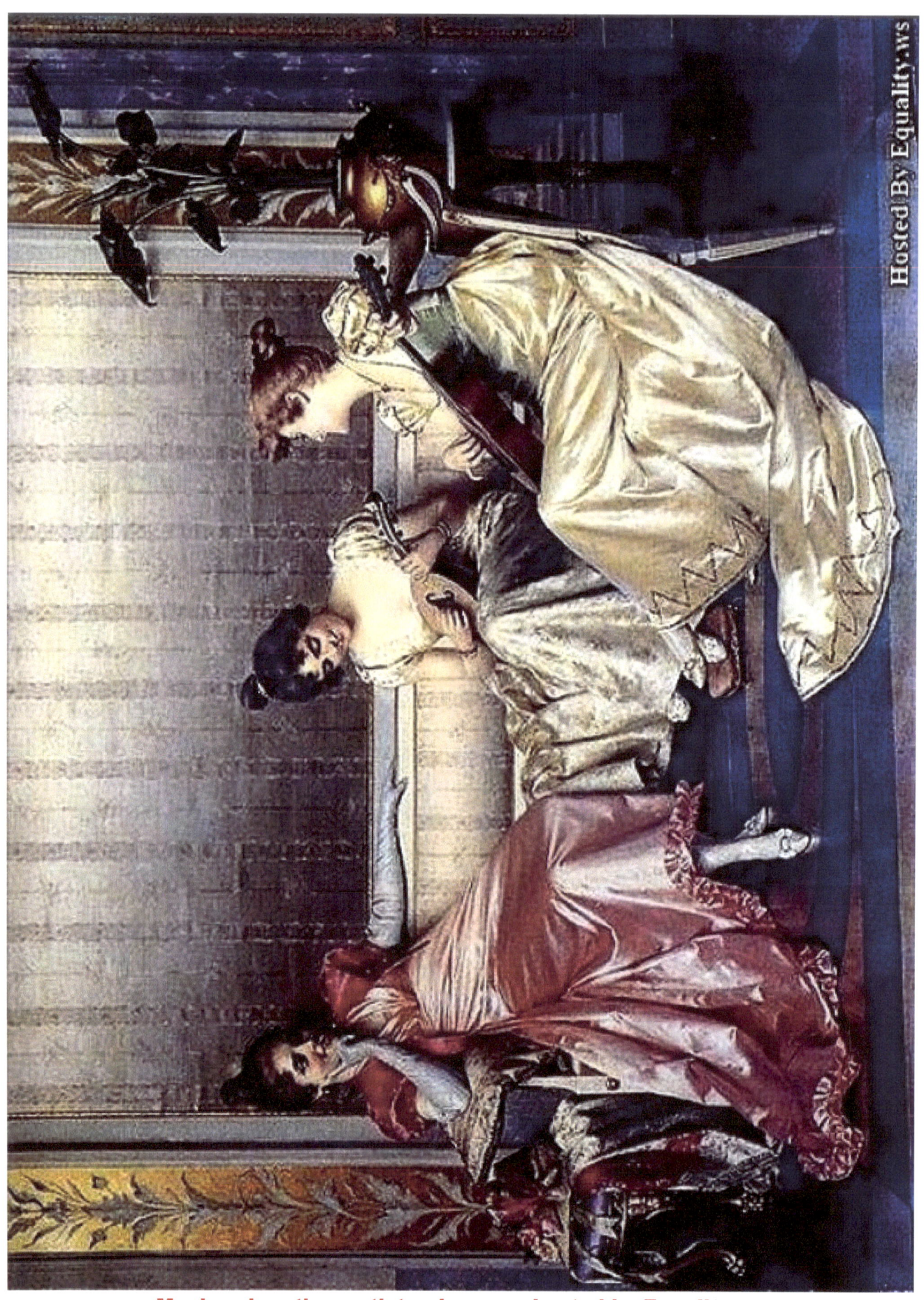

Music relaxation, artist unknown – hosted by Equality.ws

Fave Art - 15

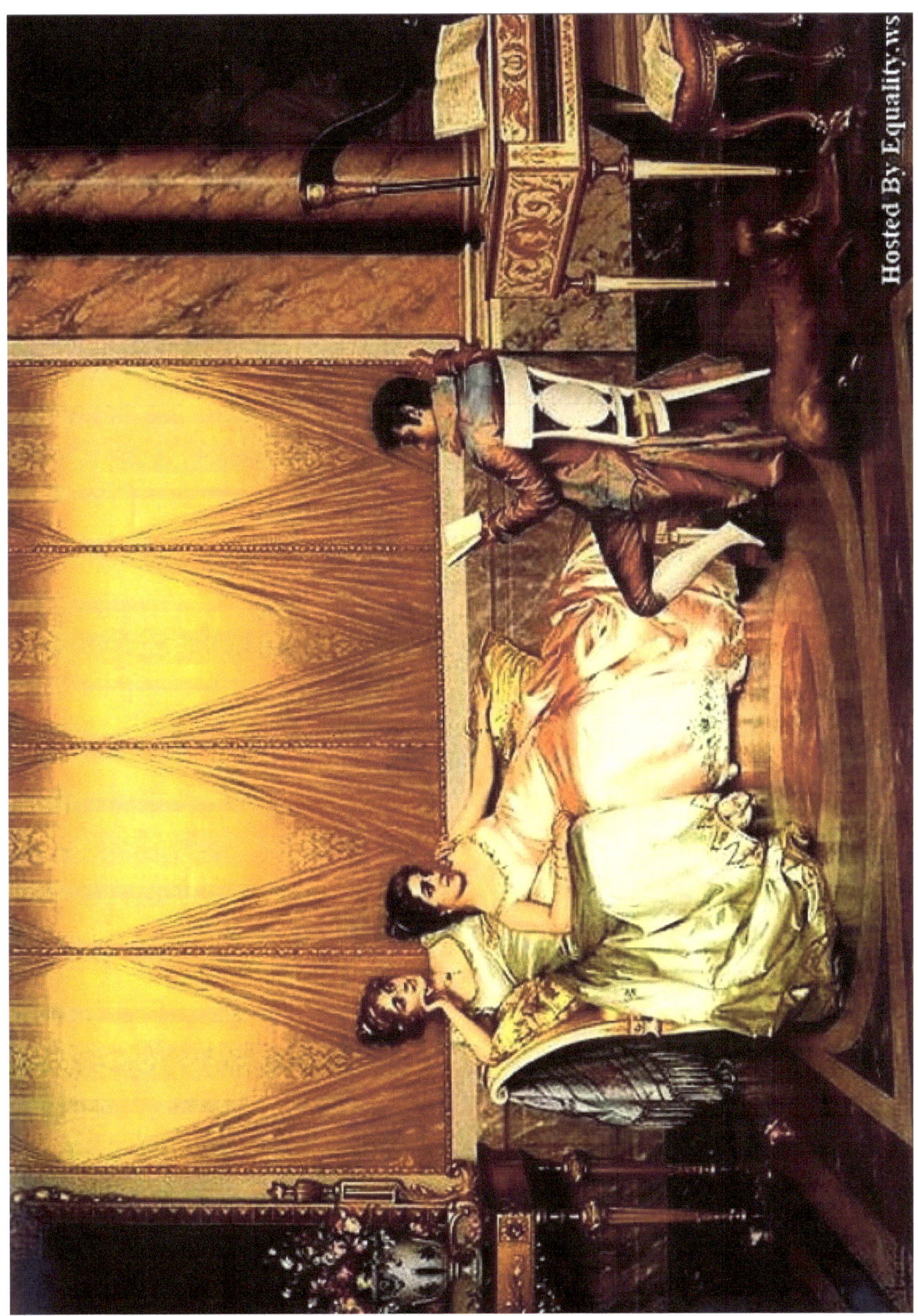

Reading Room, artist unknown – hosted by Equality.ws

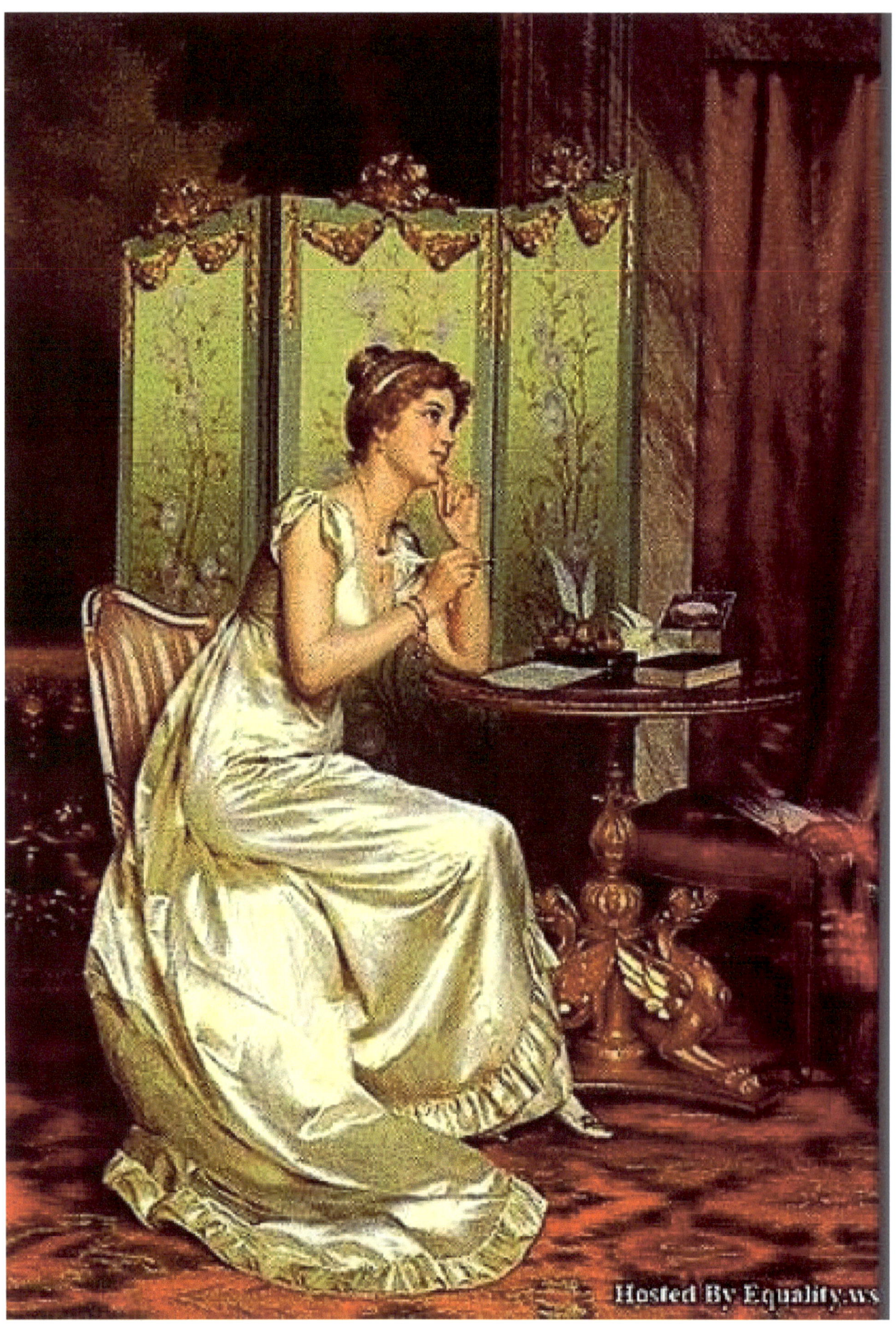

Lady writing, artist unknown – hosted by Equality.ws

Fave Art - 15

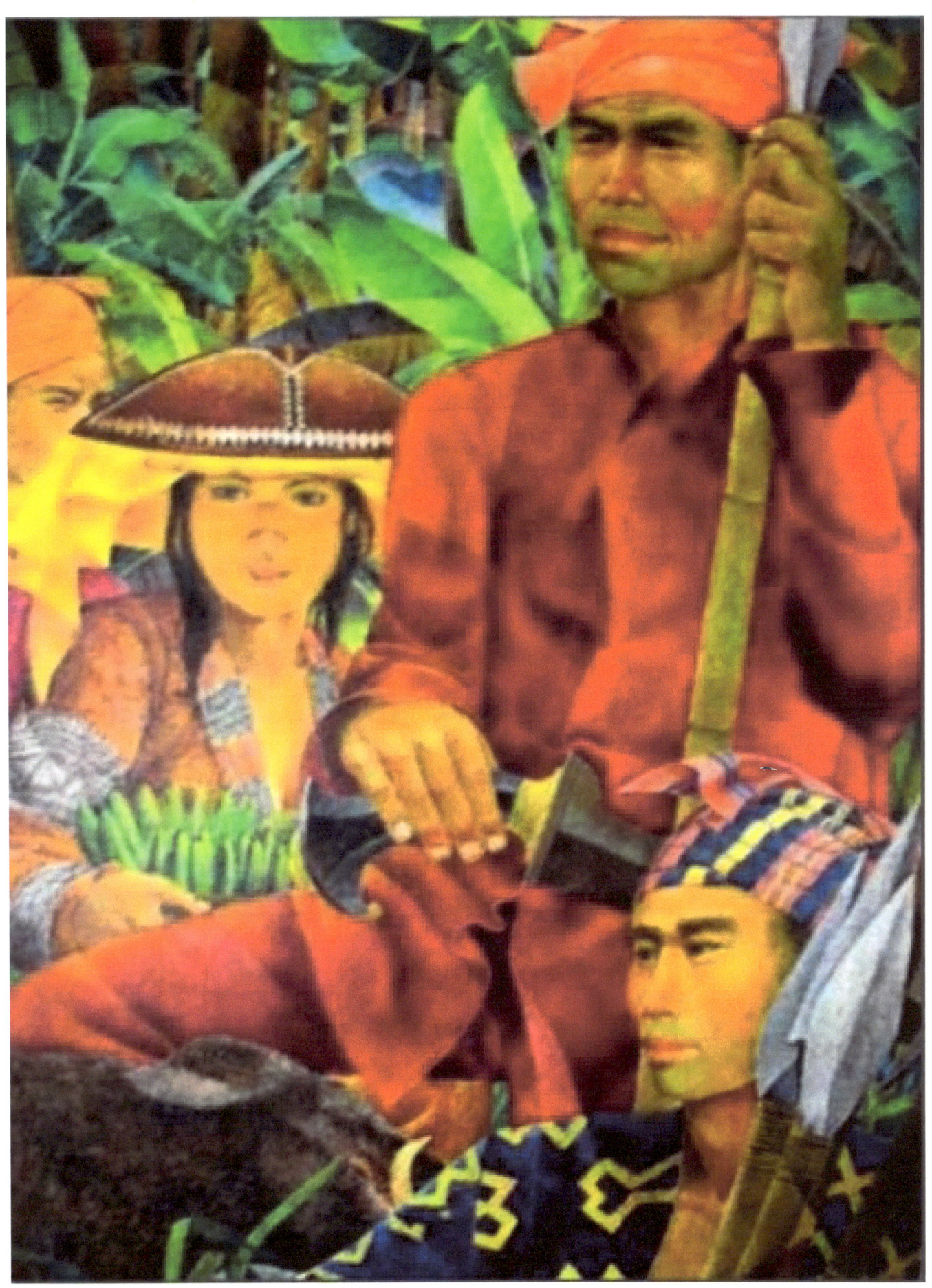

Mindanao people in Philippines, art courtesy of Percival Campoamor Cruz, a friend

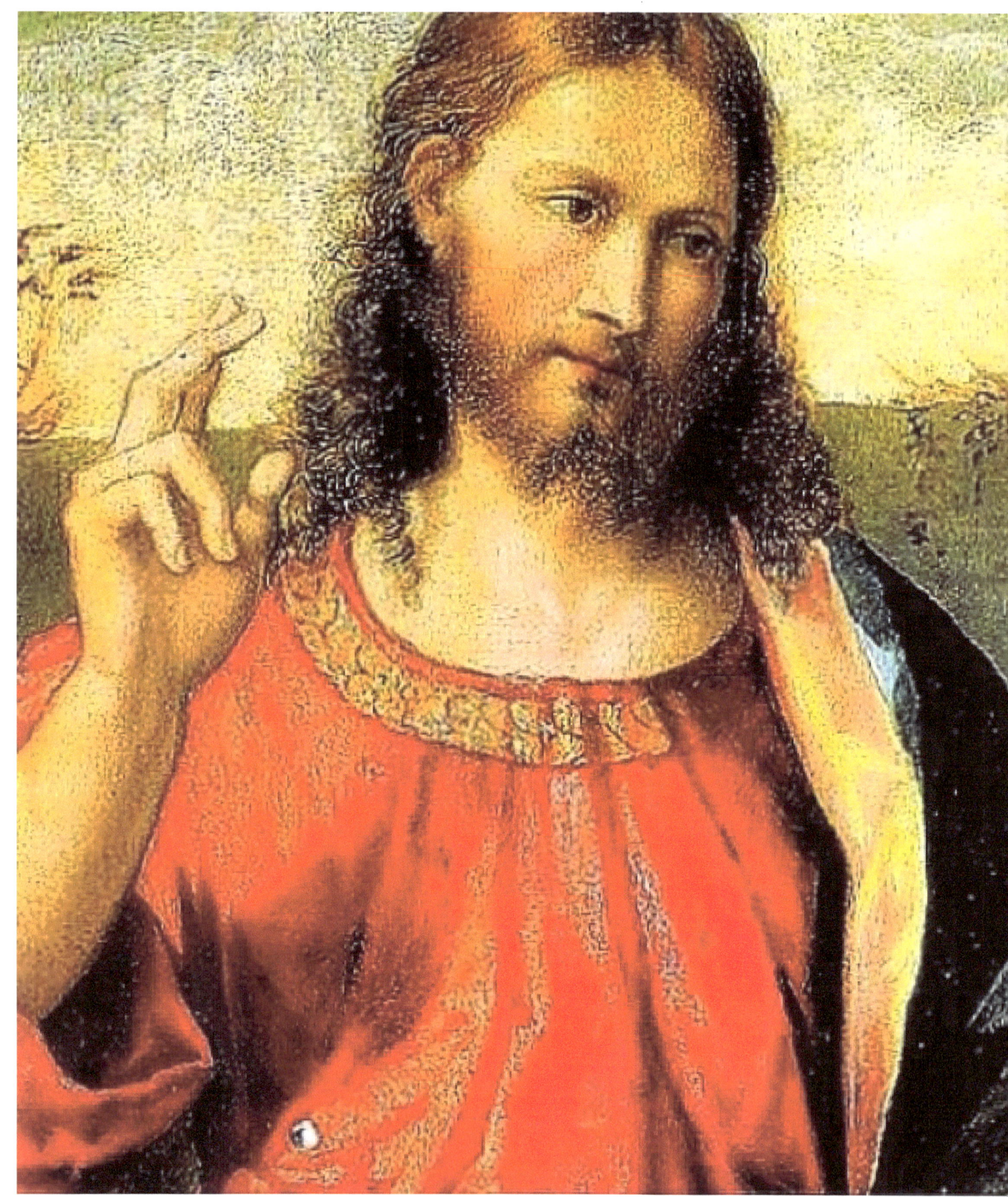

Renaissance painting of Jesus

Fave Art - 15

The Adoration of the Kings – a Renaissance painting

Fave Art - 15

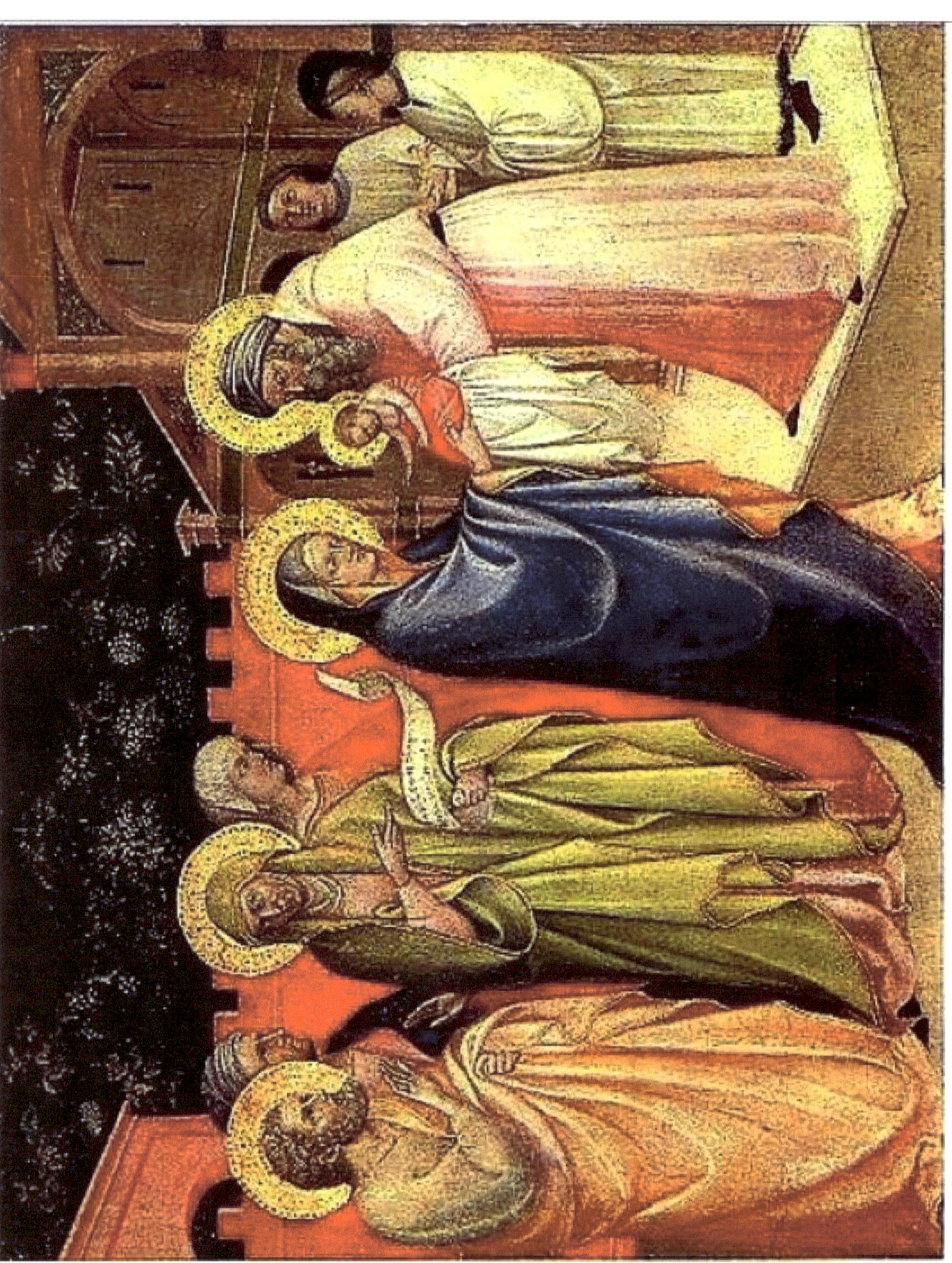

The Presentation in the Temple – Renaissance painting

The Last Supper or, The Communion of the Apostles

Luke 22: 19, 20

19 And he took bread, and gave thanks, and brake it, and gave unto them, saying, This is my body which is given for you: this do in remembrance of me.

20 Likewise also the cup after supper, saying, This cup is the new testament in my blood, which is shed for you.

Gert van (Joos van Wassenhove), The Last Supper or, The Communion of the Apostles – Circa Paris

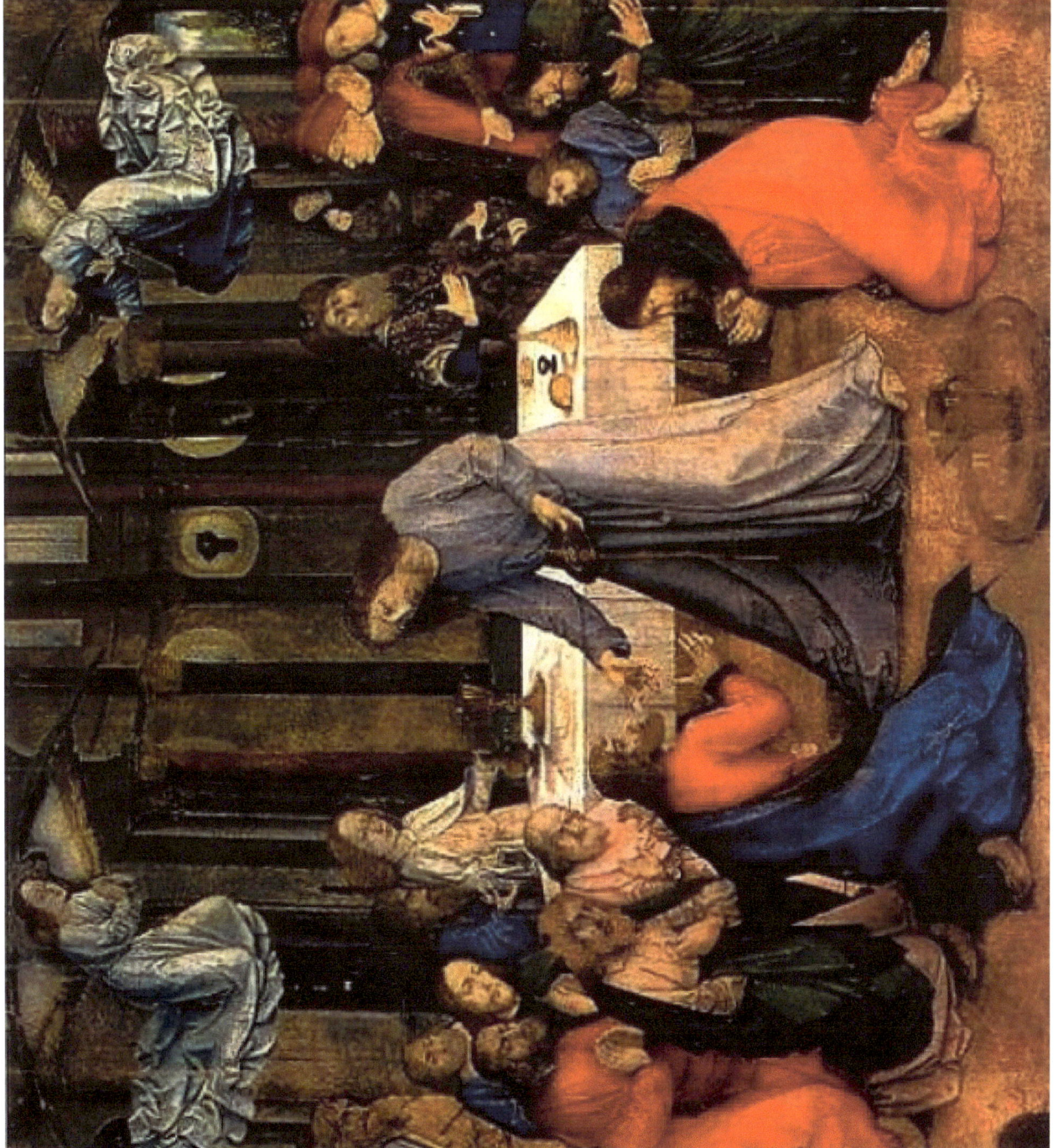

The Communion of the Apostles – Renaissance painting

Fave Art - 15

The Healing of the Blind Man – Renaissance painting

Fave Art - 15

The Transfiguration – Renaissance painting

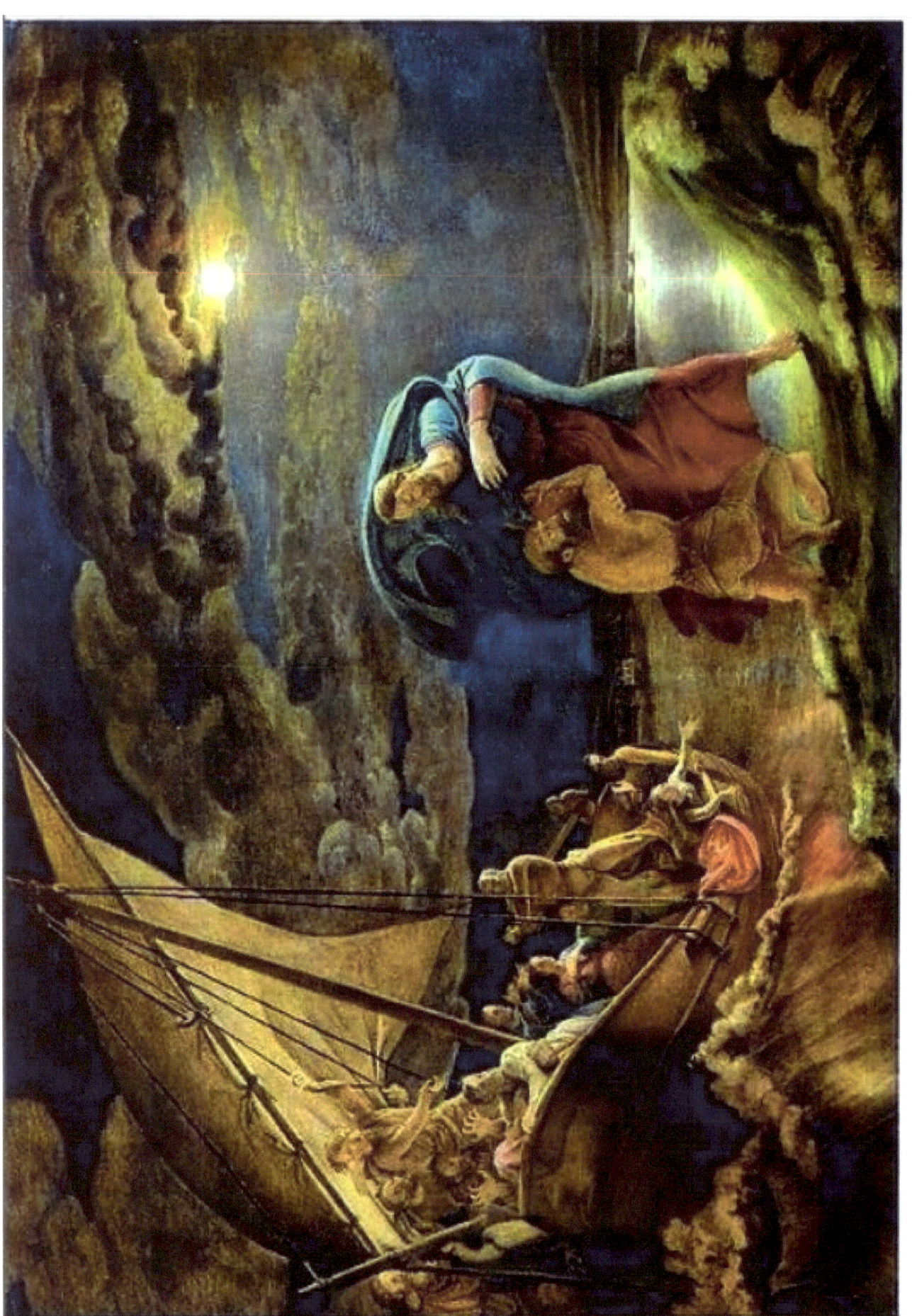

Peter Walks on Water – Renaissance painting

Fave Art - 15

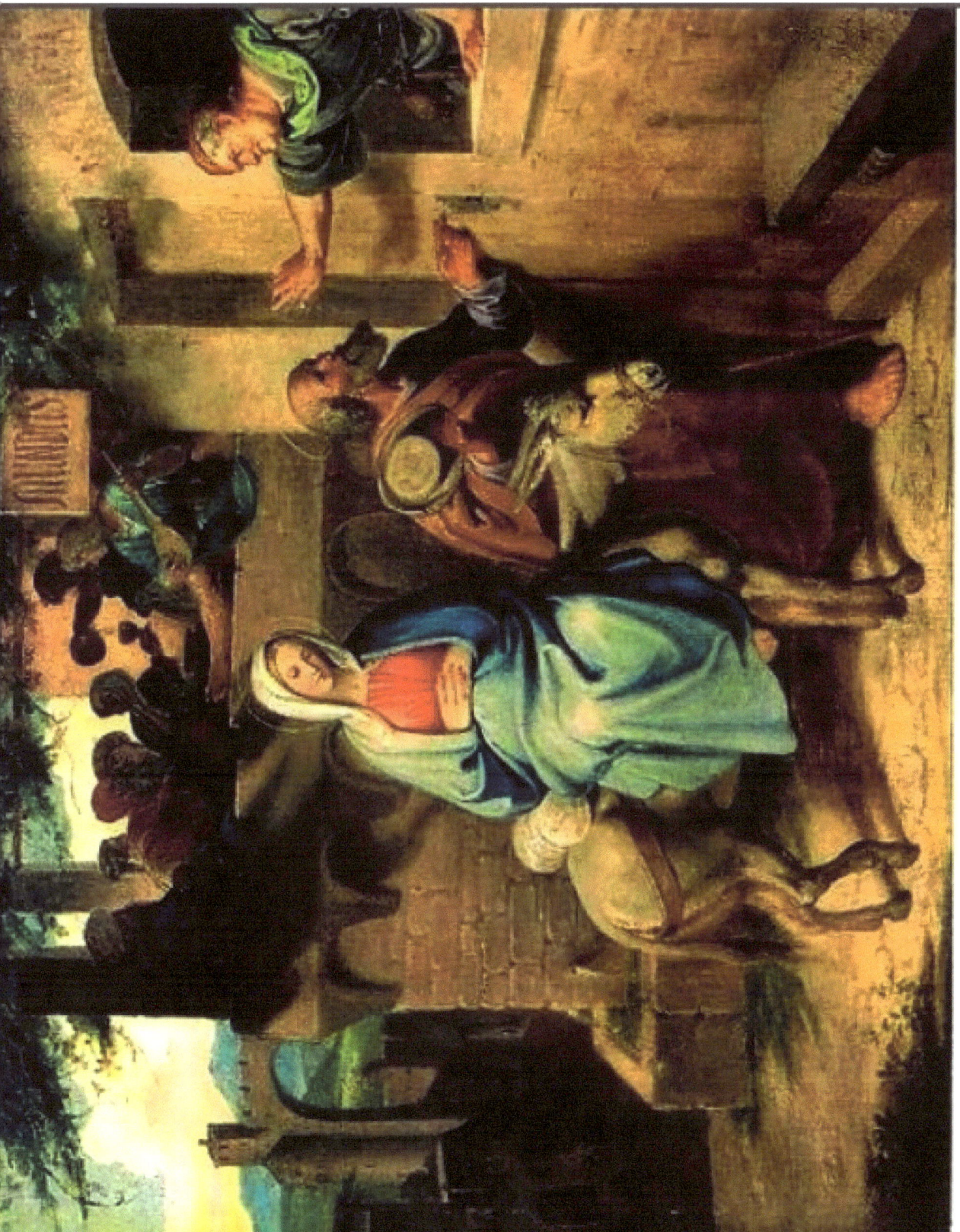

Arrival in Jerusalem – Renaissance painting

WELCOME! We hope you will enjoy this Fave Art-15 photo album of my favorite random collection of art. Photos are copied from the internet, posters, calendars, cards and art books. You may display this book as coffee table book in your living room, as conversation piece. You may give this as gift. You may cut out each page, 8.5x11 inches, for framing.

Christ on the Cross – renaissance painting

Fave Art - 15

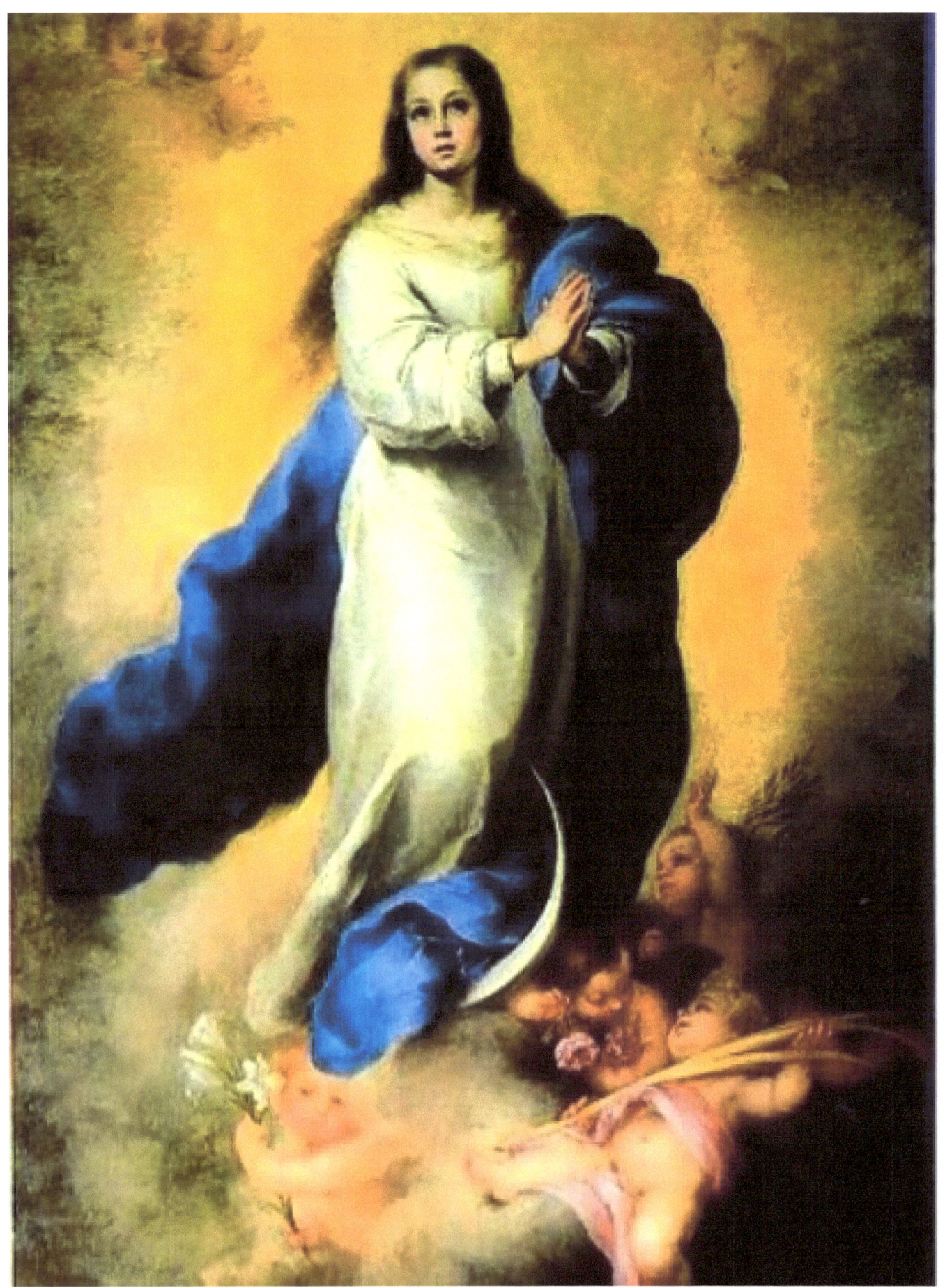

The Immaculate Conception – Renaissance painting

Fave Art - 15

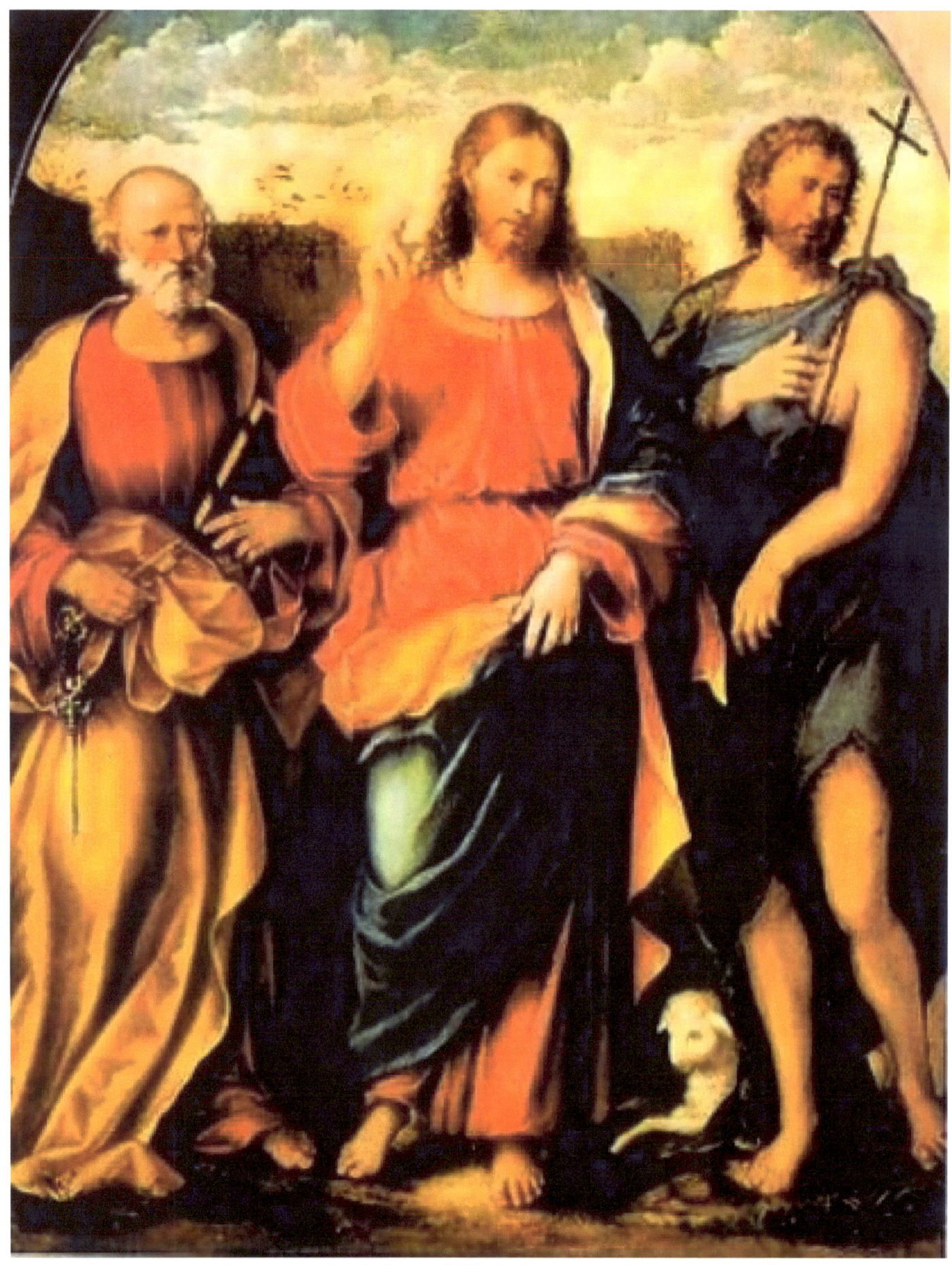

Jesus between St. John and St. Peter – Renaissance painting

Fave Art - 15

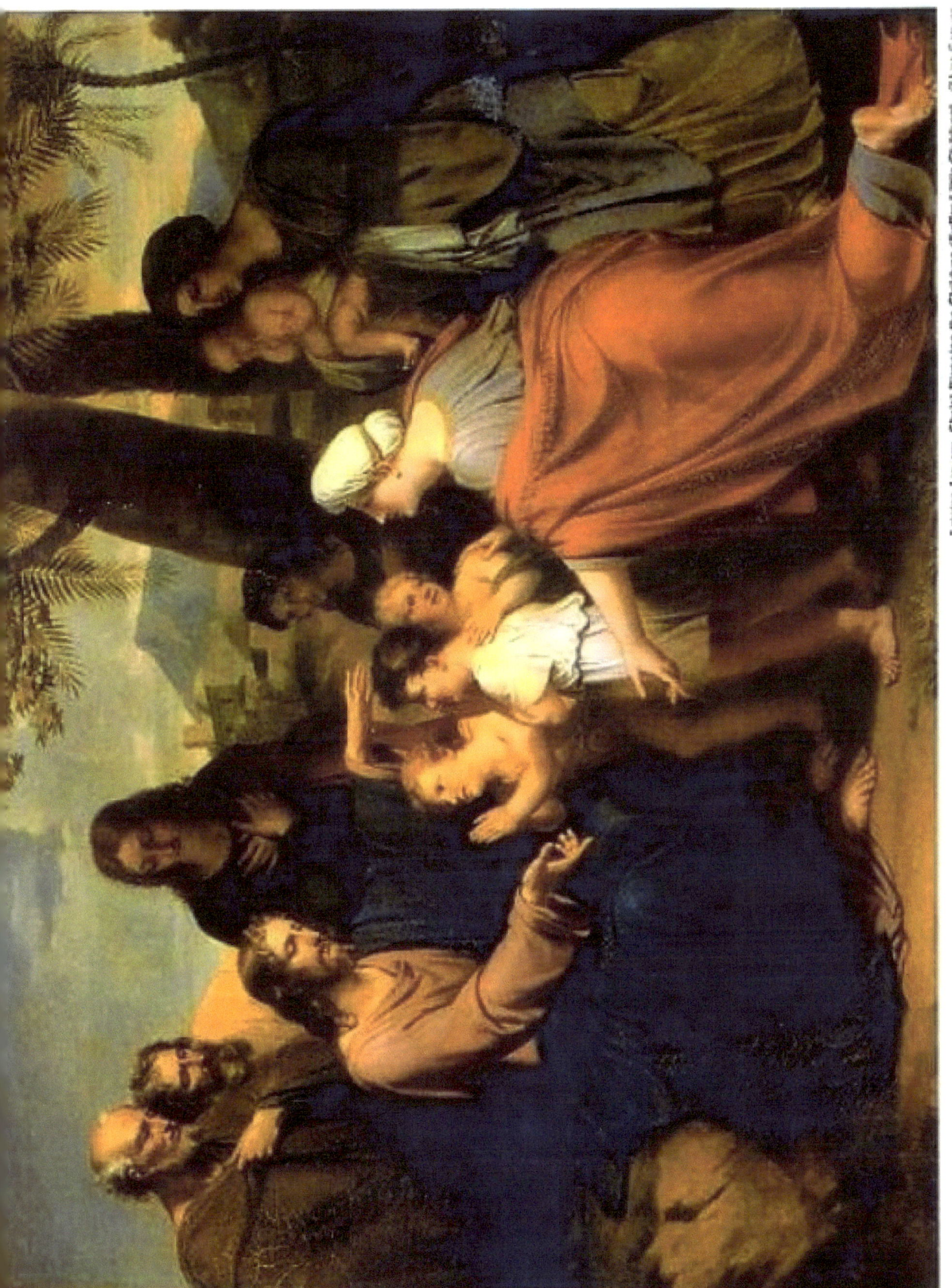

Suffer Little Children – Renaissance painting

Fave Art - 15

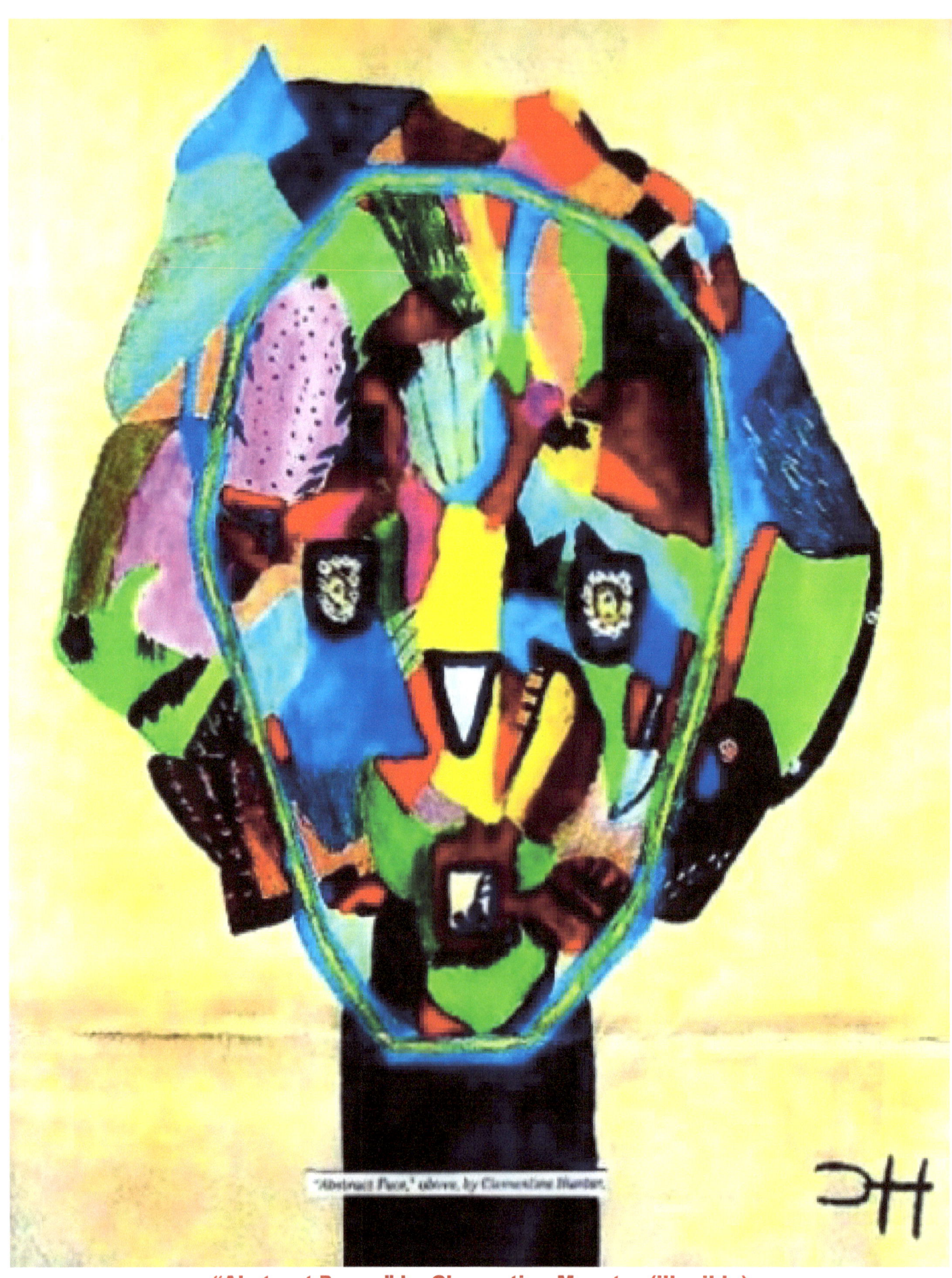

"Abstract Power" by Clementine Munster (illegible)

Fave Art - 15

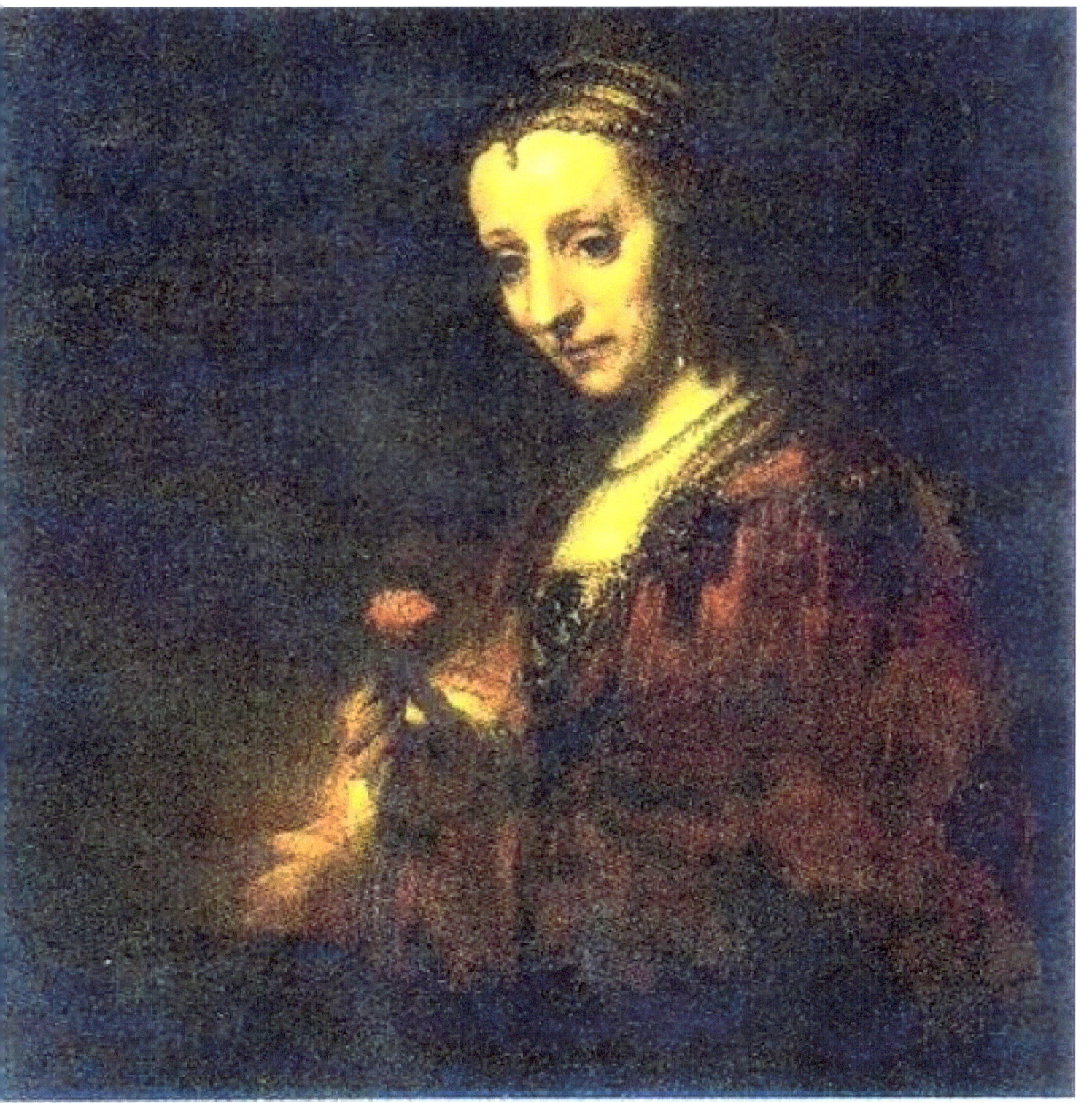

Rembrandt's "Woman With a Pink," from the early 1660s, at the Metropolitan Museum, takes on a new cast in new times.

A Rembrandt

Fave Art - 15

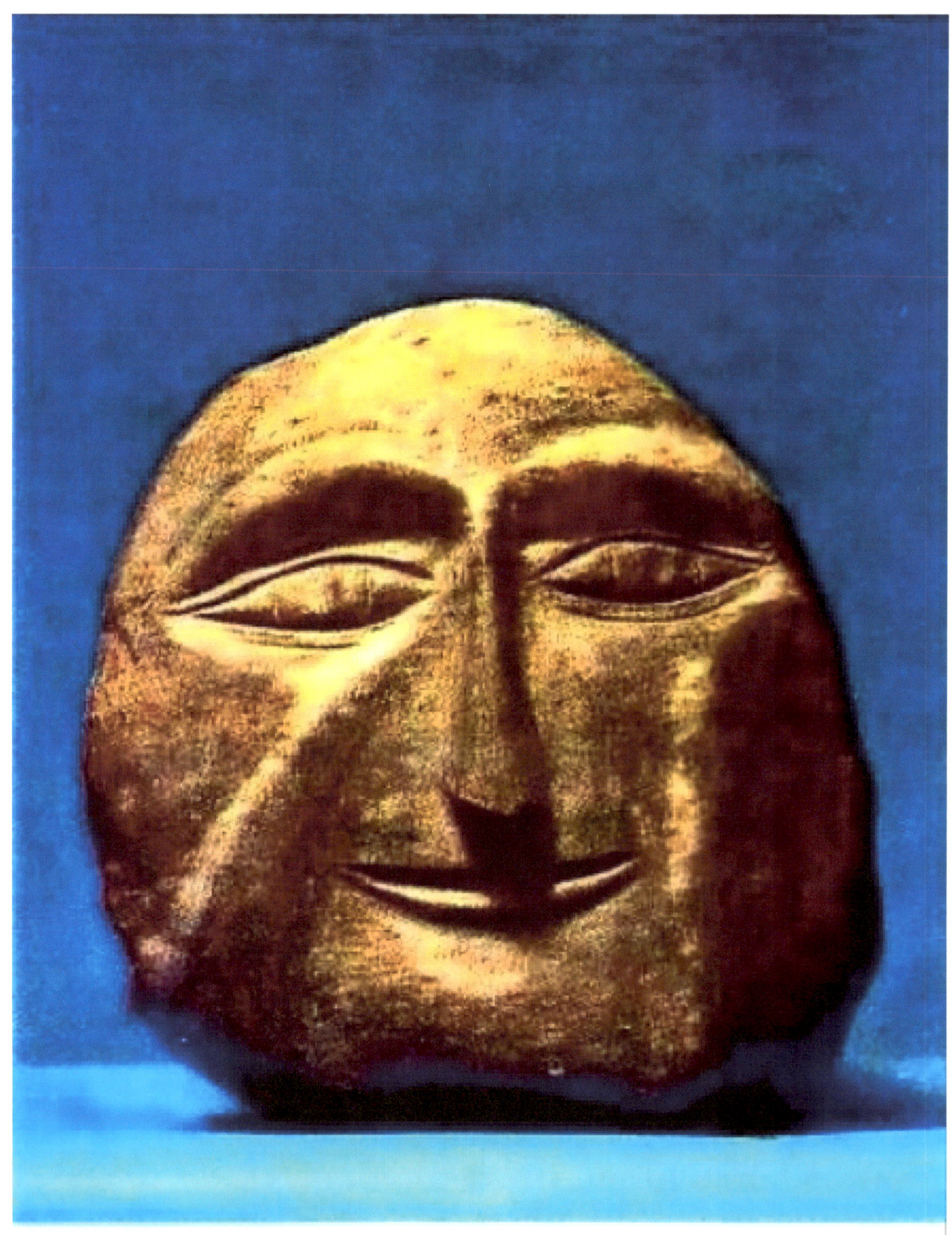

"Banded Granite Head" by Ted Ludwiczak.

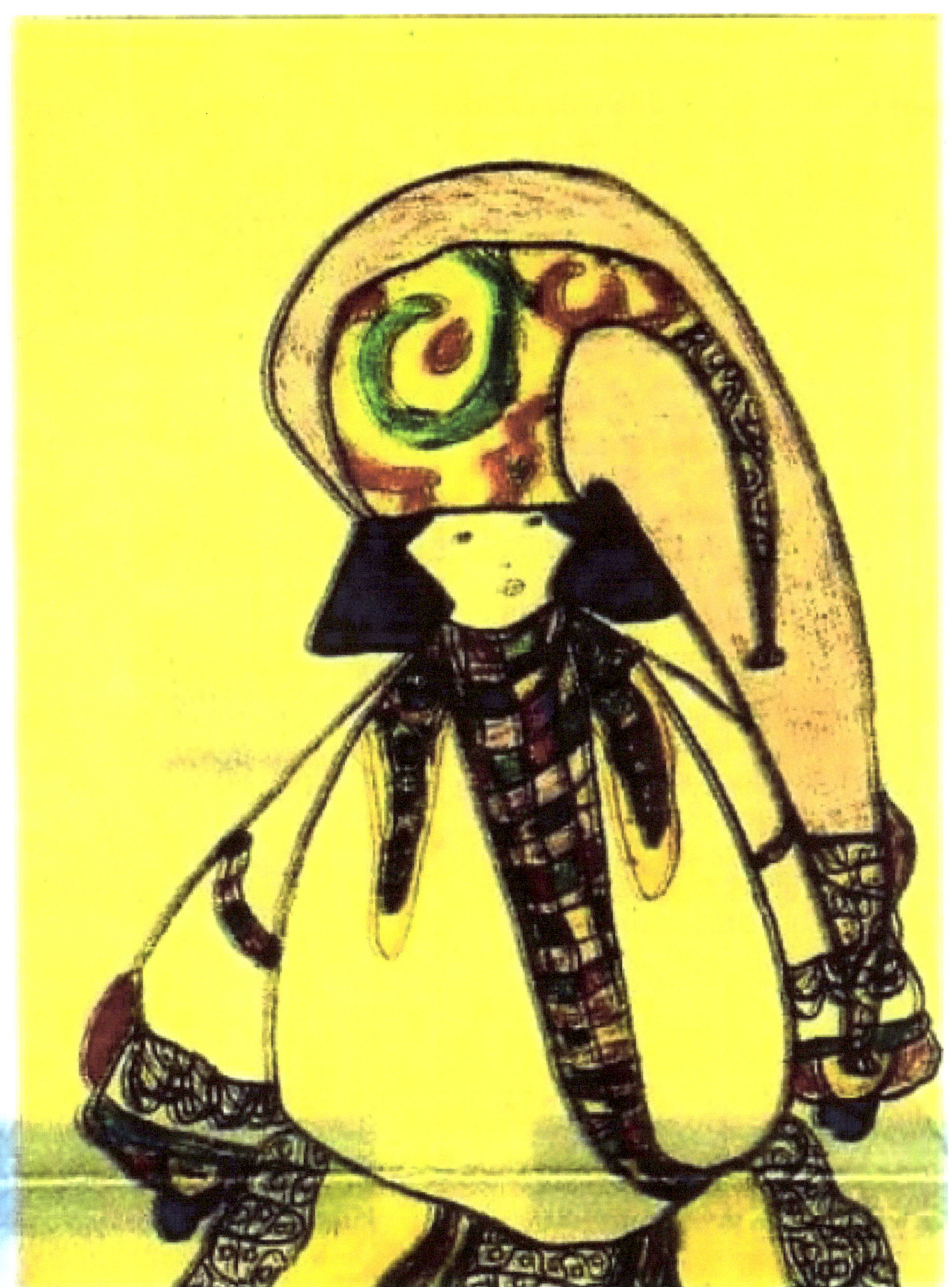

"VR 7 Untitled" (1920), in pencil and crayon on paper, by Violetta C. Raditz, who was an artist from Philadelphia.

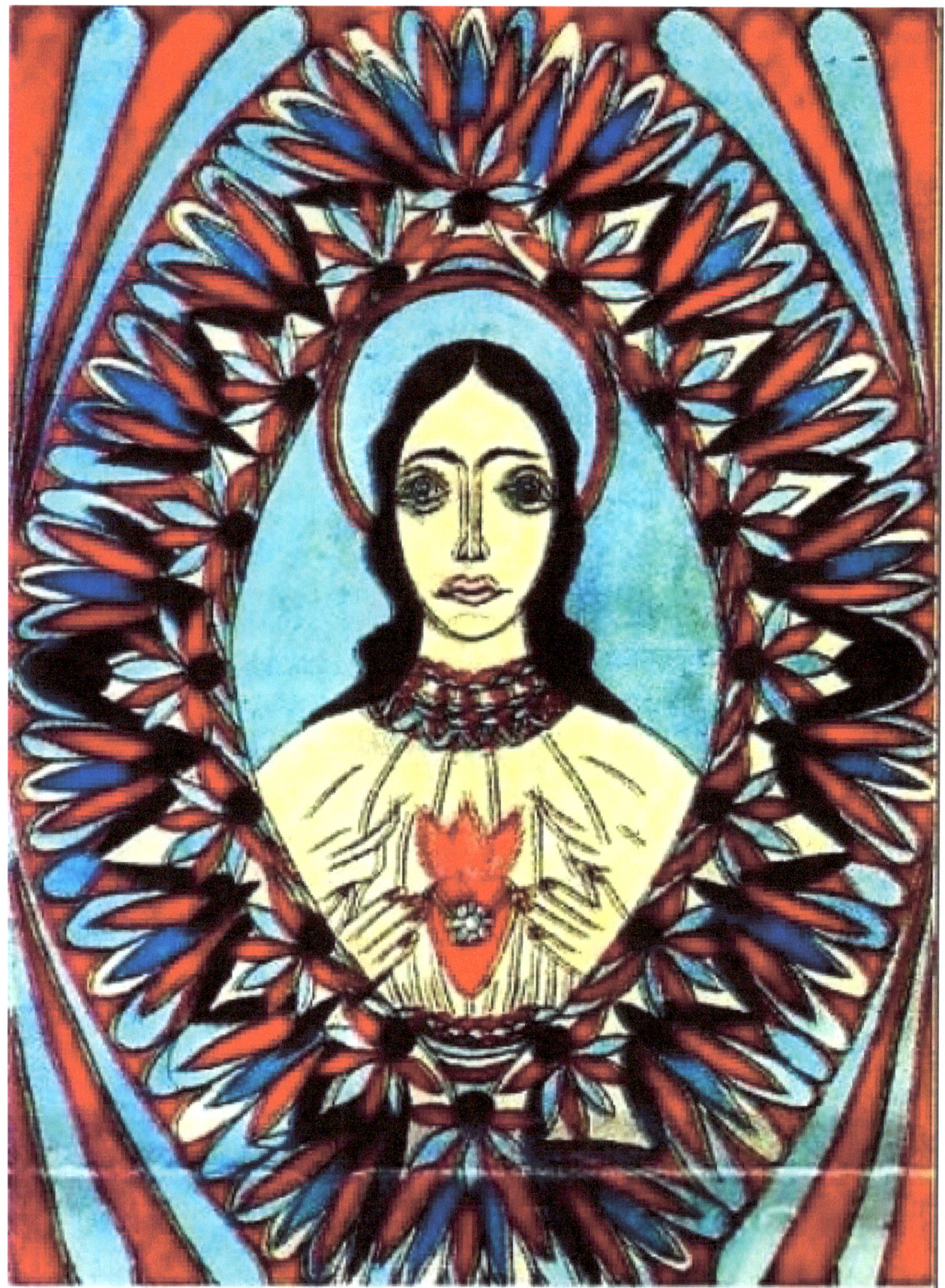

"Untitled," around 1950-65, by Stephen Palmer, a Wisconsin farmer who created shrinelike portraits of religious figures.

Fave Art - 15

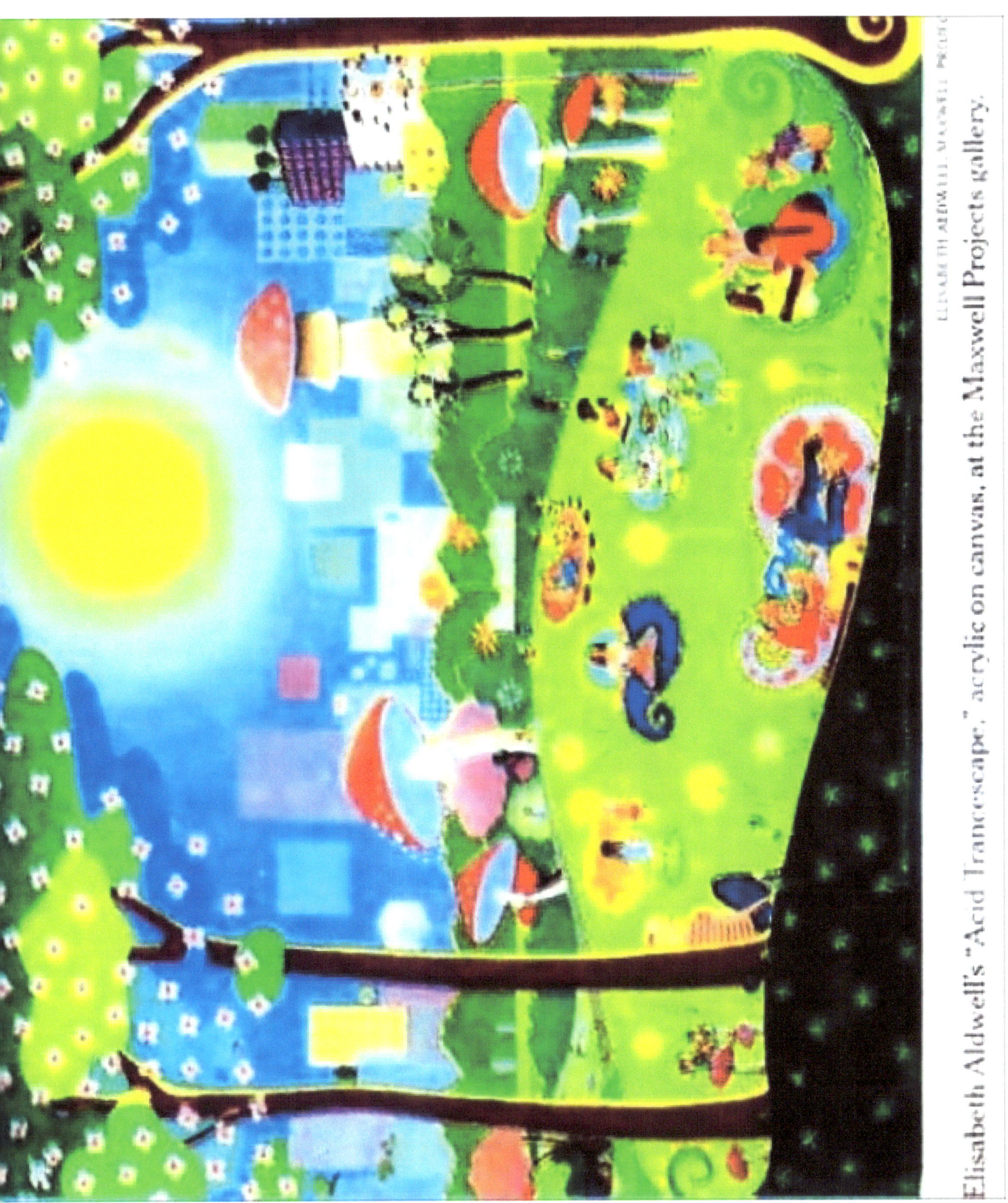

Elizabeth Aldwell – "Acid Transcape" – acrylic at Maxwell Gallery

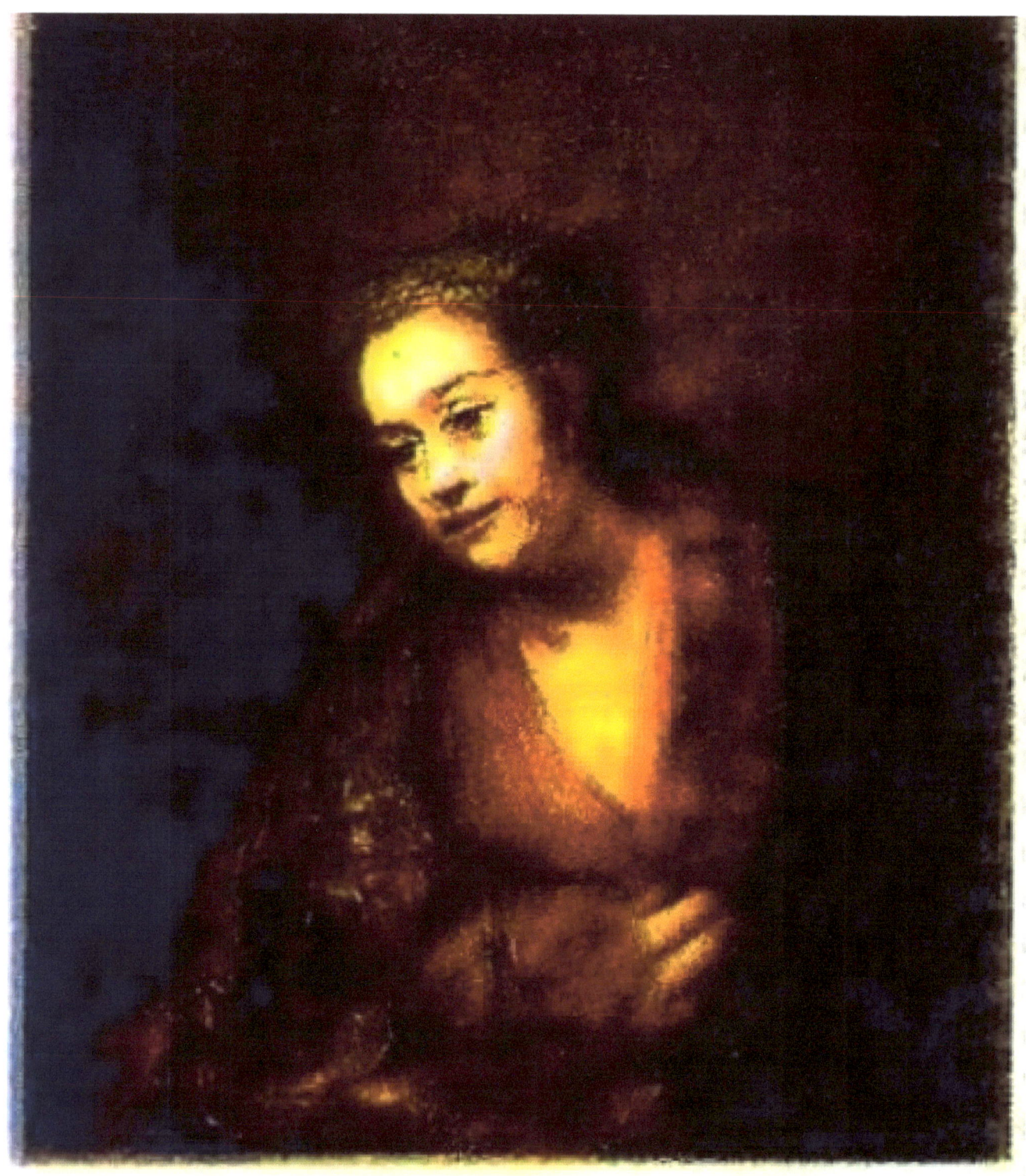

Rembrandt's portrait of a lover, Hendrickje Stoffels (1660).

Fave Art - 15

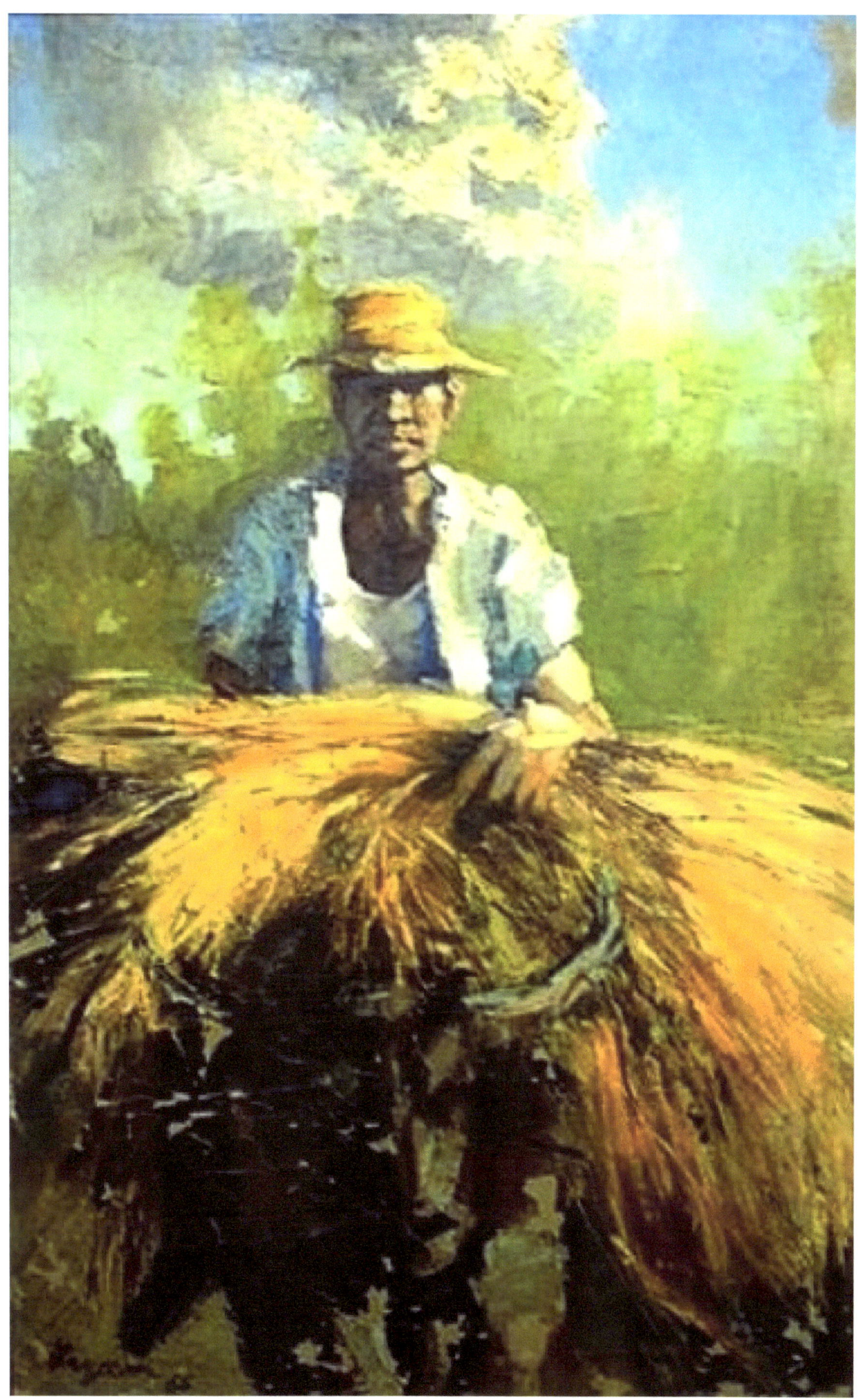

Harvest – painter and year unknown

Fave Art - 15

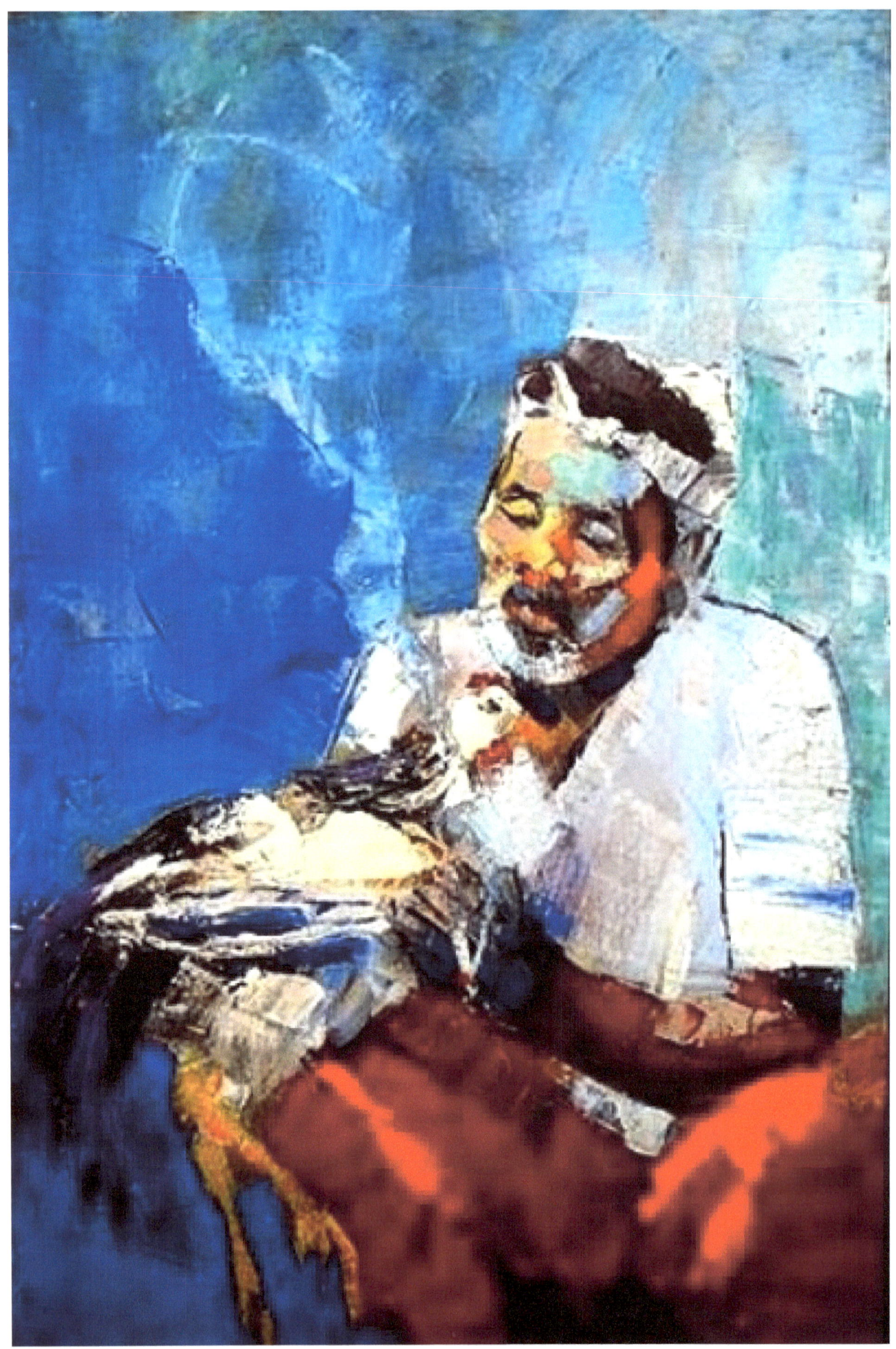

Sabungero – painter/year unknown

Fave Art - 15

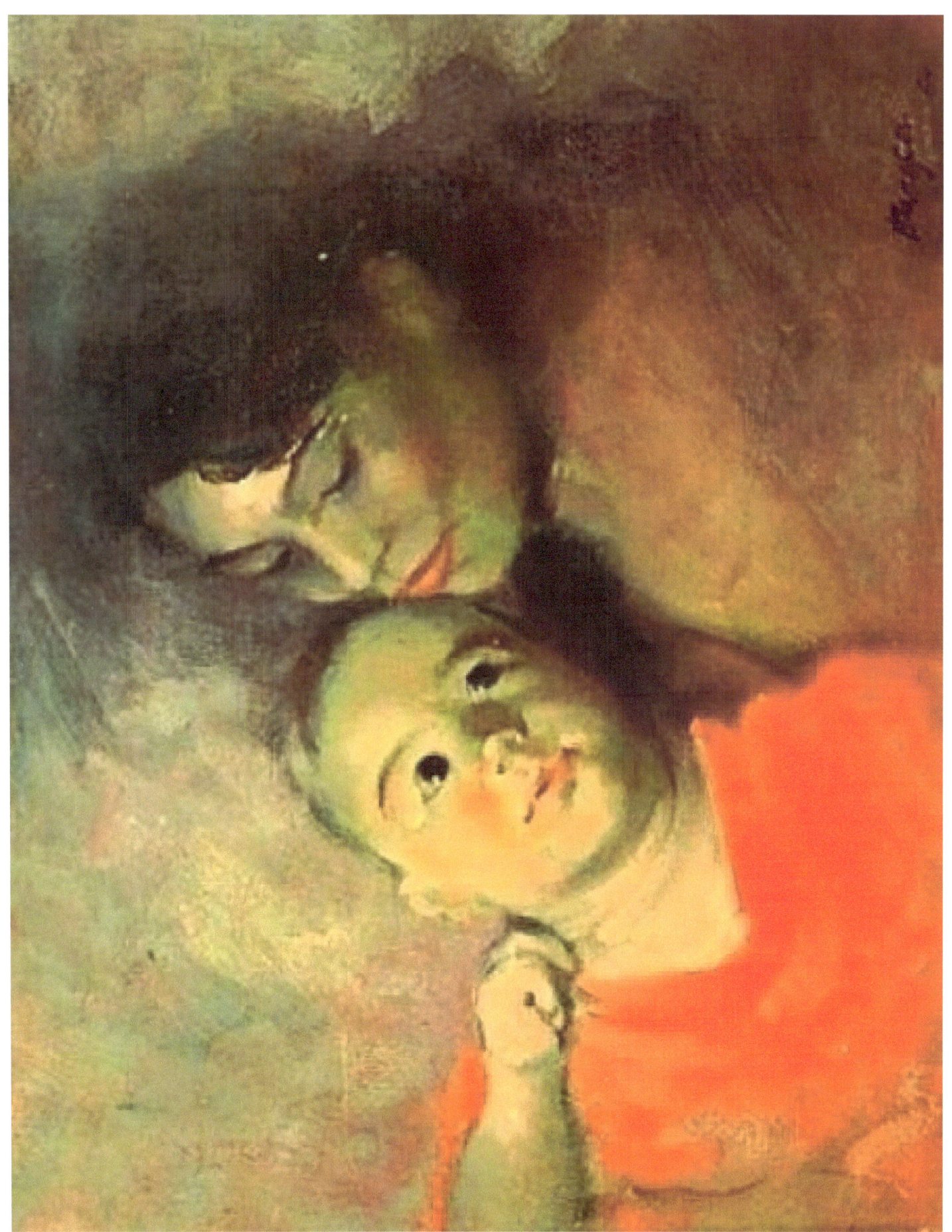

Mom & Son – Painter/year unknown

Fave Art - 15

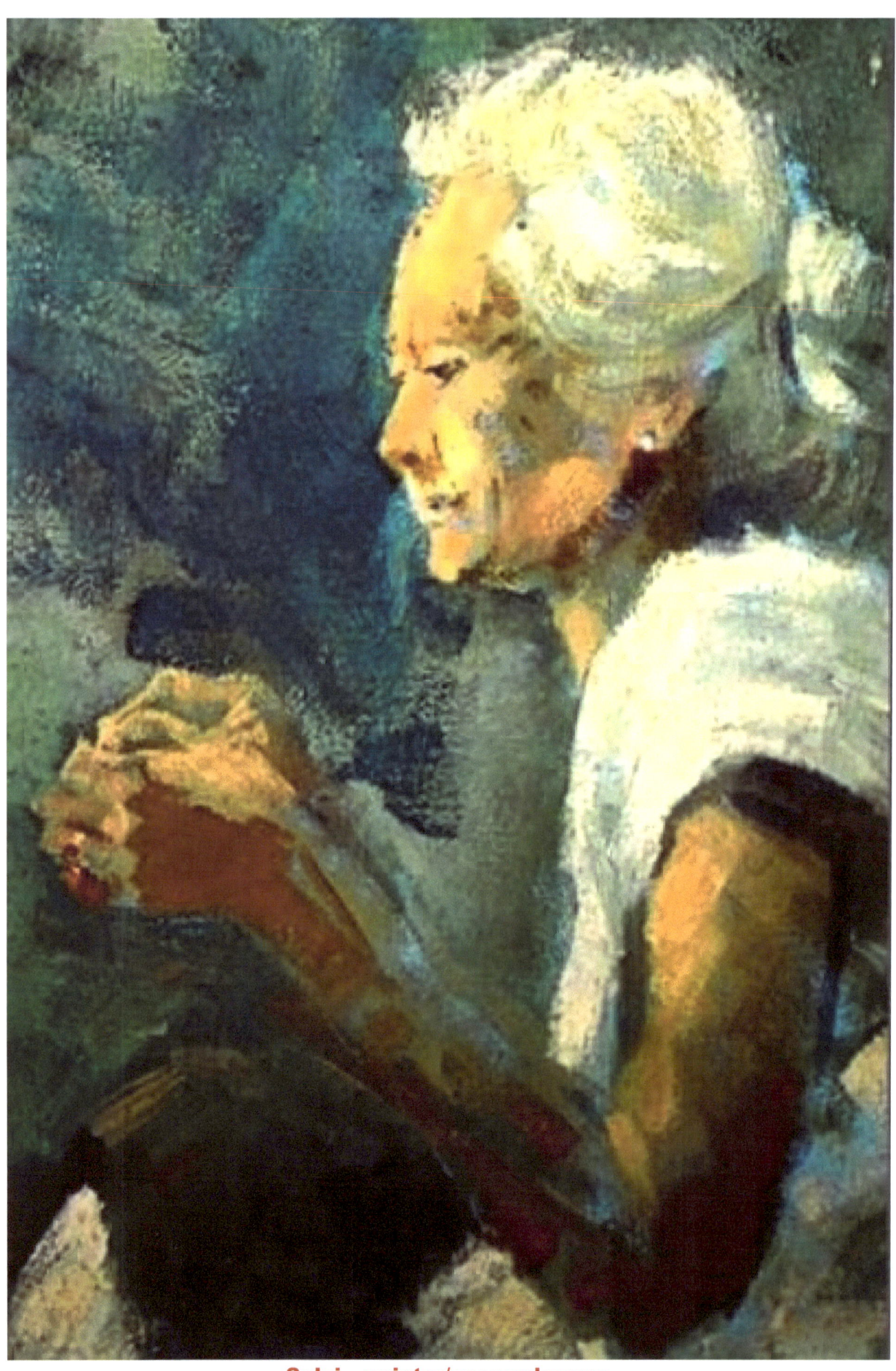

Sulsi – painter/year unknown

Fave Art - 15

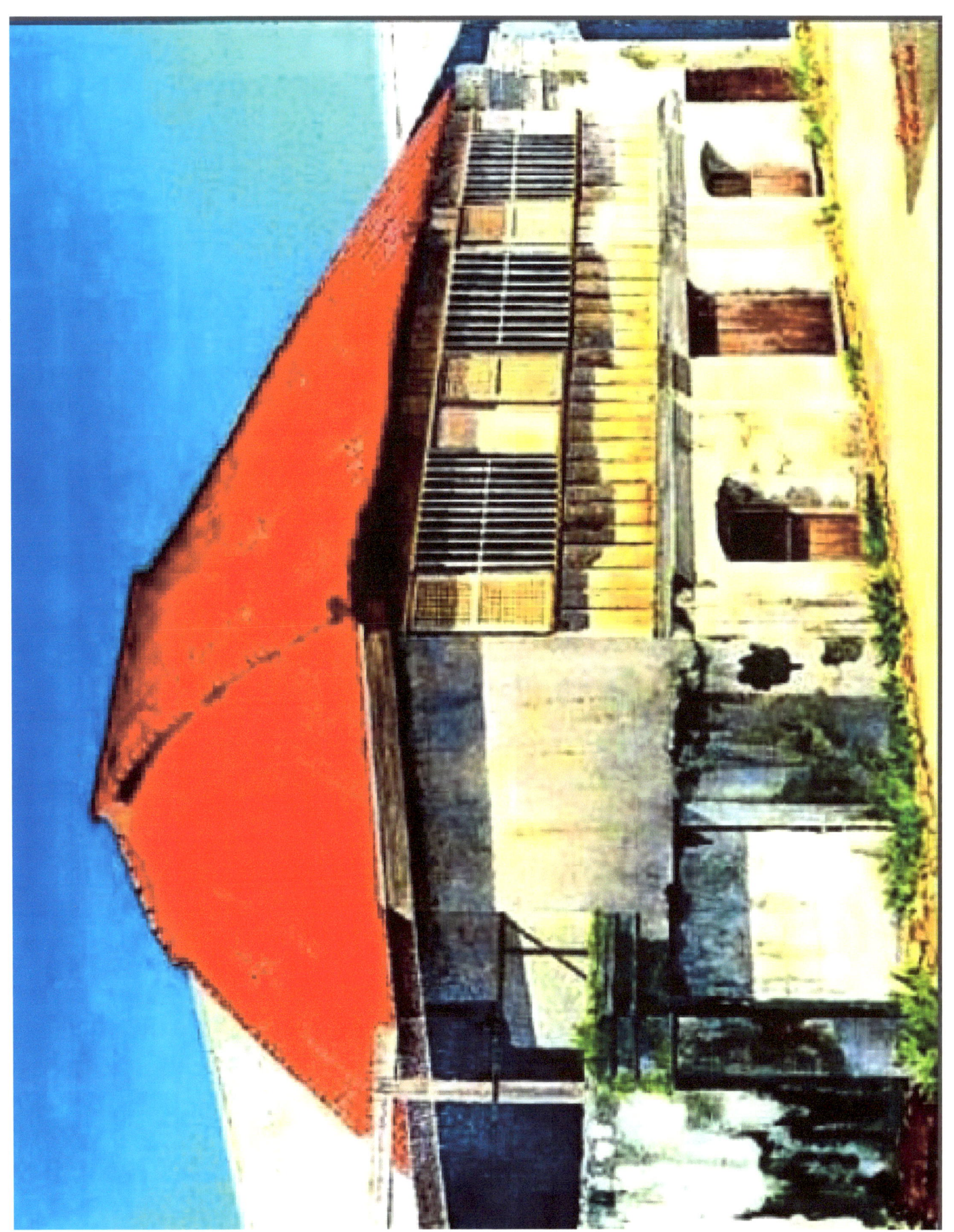

Red Roof – by Ragodon

www.ingramcontent.com/pod-product-compliance
Lightning Source LLC
Chambersburg PA
CBHW040412220526
45473CB00004B/1219